Simple Steps for Winning in Life

Exploring the Psychology of Personal, Career, Financial, and Relational Success

By Josiah Samuel Harry

Book design by Josiah S. Harry
Cover design by Josiah S. Harry

Published by CreateSpace
North Charleston, South Carolina

ISBN: 978-1508599555

Contents

Part I: Personal Success i

You Are Amazing! 1

We're All Chasing After Something 4

Find a Mentor or Coach 6

Win Because You Matter 8

Regret vs. Guilt 11

Take Control of Your Personal Brand 14

Difficult Does Not Mean Impossible 16

Commit to the Grind 18

Old-Fashioned Hard Work 20

I Believe in Luck 22

Psychology Application 24

Part II: Career Success 28

Education Matters 30

College Is Not For Everyone 32

An Entrepreneurial Mindset 34

Too Stubborn To Fail 40

Success Is Not Easily Attained 42

You Are Fired! 44

Personal Branding 47

Networking 50

How to Dominate a Competitive Industry 52

The Kevin Durant Effect 55

Psychology Application 58

Part III: Financial Success 60

Wealthy Mindset 62

Start with a Budget 64

Spend Less Than You Earn 66

Save, Save, Save 68

Avoiding Debt 70

Wage Slave or Employee? 72

Start Your Own Business 76

Choosing the Right Career Path 78

Laughing to the Bank 80

Putting It All Together 83

Psychology Application 85

Part IV: Relational Success 87

Dirty Laundry 89

Man Up 98

Woman Up 102

Mate-Retention Strategy 105

The Gold Fish Mentality 108

Tabula Rasa 112

$ Bling Bling $ 114

Call the Cops 117

Social Media and Relationships 123

Relational Intimacy 125

Psychology Application 127

Part V: Self-Empowerment 131

You Are Phenomenal! 134

Do Not Follow Your Passion 137

Execution Is Worshiped! 140

You Owe It To Yourself.. 143

Do These Things Before Going To Bed...................... 145

I'll Just Watch You Drown.. 147

A Fate Worse Than Death 153

Motivated To Do Something You Love...................... 156

Nobody Cares About Your Story Until You Win 159

Go Fund Me_The New Hustle..................................... 162

You Do Deserve Life's Best.. 166

About the Author 169

"Aha" Moments.. 171

Budget Worksheet 183

Part I: Personal Success

What is success? How do we measure it? And what does it look like? Does success mean owning a beachfront home, a few exotic cars, a luxury yacht and a personal helicopter? Perhaps success implies gainful employment and steady income? Could it be that success is determined by a person's happiness quotient?

There are countless ways to measure or define success, and the reality is, people are in active pursuit of this elusive phenomenon. Each of the status artifacts listed above is impressive. Do you know of anyone who would not like to have steady income, a nice place to rest her head and a nice car to drive?

Even so, while those symbols are often viewed as being indicative of success, I would put forth that they are simply markers, or things we collect on the path to success. Material possession or income level is not a true measurement of success.

So, how else could success be defined? Within the context of this book, success, i.e., winning, is about creating, studying and exploring a world that enables a person to find fulfillment. Success is that overwhelming feeling that comes from doing what you love. Success is also about taking advantage of an opportunity in the lifetime of the opportunity.

Most importantly, success or winning is fun, holistic and sustainable. Winning is being aware of, and comfortable with one's authentic self—it's about figuring out the most productive and happiest way to live.

You Are Amazing!

What matters most to you, and why?

I mean, what really, really turns you on? What is it that gets your juices flowing? If your life were amazing, what would it look like? And what could you do to make this very moment a memorable one?

Well, you have to be deliberate. Deliberate about what, though? Is it believing in yourself, selecting realistic goals; defining those goals; hard work and effort; embracing setbacks; or planning ahead? I am certain that you've tried one or more of those steps. So, what's the problem? Better yet, what is the solution?

For starters, it is important to note that *there are no secrets to success.* If you truly want to be amazing, then you must accept that **YOU ARE AMAZING!** Let that thought sink in....

When an eagle is about to grace the sky with its majestic presence—whether to exercise its wings or hunt for its next meal, it does not question its "eagleness," meaning, its essence and ability. No, no. The eagle simply leans over its perch and take to the air to accomplish its mission.

The principle here is to tell you that greatness lives within you. You simply need to activate it. And one of the best ways to step into a phenomenal existence is to **surround yourself with amazing people**.

A few years ago, I created a make or break list. I took out a piece of paper and divided it into two columns. One column listed the people who would help me improve my life, and the other column listed those who would drag me down.

The people whom I determined could improve my life, I lived and breathed in their shadows, meaning that I spent as much time around them as possible. I asked questions and implemented actionable strategies that helped me achieve my goals. Conversely, as it relates to the people who weren't winning, I spent no more than five minutes around them.

If you want to experience unparalleled success, then build and utilize your connection capital. Surround yourself with people who are winning—people who will challenge you and hold you accountable even if it makes you uncomfortable—the kind of people who expect and demand greatness!

We're All Chasing After Something

We're all chasing after something, right? Comfort, access, security. A place to belong. God, community, kinship. A dream, success, a career, status artifacts. Someone's approval, someone's attention, someone's affirmation. Love, happiness, respect, friends. An idea of how life is supposed to be.

We have been told that whatever we plan to pursue, we should begin with the end in mind. But what if this chase has no end – no definitive direction or destination? What if our pursuit is a journey into *becoming?*

I know…becoming "what?" Well, just *becoming*—a journey through liminality.

I get it. It's human nature to want to solve the unknown. What if, however, there isn't anything to be solved? What if what we're really searching for is not an answer, but a question?

It is not the question you are thinking about. It is the ultimate question. It is the question that asks us to give up something. One of the mysteries of the universe is to give and take. That's the flow of life. The path we're on requires that we give up something in order to receive what the universe has in store for us.

In order to get, we must first be willing to give. We must pay it forward by making our concentric circle—those closest to us, better. We cannot receive the universe's benediction if we refuse to *let go*—to let go of pride and selfishness.

Once we *give* ourselves permission to be free from those things, we are also making space for the Infinite Intelligence to deposit its gifts into our lives.

Most of us are chasing after something much bigger than us. But in order to achieve our dreams, goals and aspirations, we must not allow selfish interests to weigh us down. We must be deliberate and insistent in looking out for and preserving the right and well-being of others as we are for our own.

Find a Mentor or Coach

Every year, a few marathon swimmers drown. That seems odd as these are trained, experienced swimmers, much stronger than the average swimmer. The problem though is that during their marathon swims, these swimmers are hit repeatedly with waves, and after time, they begin to tire and start *swimming down* - with their heads staying longer and longer in the water until they eventually drown.

Why do they "swim down?" They swim down because the water is calmer beneath the surface, with no attacking waves. What would have helped these swimmers to stay alive and reach their goal? A spotter, remaining close by in a boat would have certainly helped.

The primary role of the spotter is to stay close to the swimmers, ensuring that they are keeping their heads above the water so the swimmers can finish the race.

How many spotters [mentors or coaches] do you have in your life? Have you developed meaningful relationships with a network of individuals who can help you recognize and develop your growth opportunities, and discover and build on your strengths?

In order to experience personal success, it necessitates having moral fiber, resolve, and mental stamina. Even so, while those are awesome qualities, they are not enough. In other words, personal success is really not that personal in that it always involves other people who provide a learning context to help guide your decision-making.

So, never underestimate the value of a good spotter!

Win Because You Matter

One day, it happened. I found myself caught in the mire of life's daily grind—living the grandest of illusions; meaning, enriching the lives of others, e.g., employers, religion, family and friends, even while I struggled to create momentum in my own life. I found myself waking up every day with the feeling of emptiness, with everything staring me in the face except passion, contentment and purpose. After years of gathering mere morsels from the smorgasbord of life, I finally got to the point where I was sick and tired of running on empty emotionally, physically, spiritually and socioeconomically.

You too might have been an avid participant of this grandest of illusions: waking up in the morning, showering, getting dressed, eating breakfast, going off to work or school…coming back home, maybe taking another shower, eating dinner, cuddling the TV's remote control, or surfing the Internet, then going off to bed—only to wake up the next day and repeat the same thing all over again.

If you have ever felt this way, I want to let you know that your life does not have to continue on that road to nowhere. You do not have to spend the rest of your life in misery, unhappiness, and/or dysfunction—peering at other people's success and happiness. Instead, you can create and shape your own reality and success under your terms and conditions. You can choose to fulfill your passions. So, how do you transition from where you are to where you'd like to be?

First, change your environment. Yes, that might mean leaving some family and friends behind. Secondly, absorb inspiration daily. Study the lives of successful people and find ways to integrate their methods and systems into your own experiences. One of my favorite books that address "how to" is, *The Click Moment: Seizing Opportunity in an Unpredictable World* by Frans Johansson. Another book that shows you how to transform your limitations into your greatest competitive advantages is *The Power of Broke* by Daymond John.

Thirdly, write out your dreams, passions and goals. Finally, once you have written down your goals, begin implementing them. If you do not know where to begin, then ask someone who is winning. Some of you might be saying, "I don't know anyone who is winning." Well, go out of your way and find those persons. Call them and email them. Be persistent.

Remember, winning ultimately depends on one person believing and doing – and that's YOU!

Regret vs. Guilt

Everyone has regrets. They are part of the human experience. Life is filled with uncertainties and unpredictable events, and in the midst of those uncertainties and events we sometimes inadvertently screw something up. Shit happens! Here's my question. If regrets are indeed a fact of life, then why do we work so hard at avoiding them? And should we avoid regrets?

Rather than avoiding regrets, I think there are times when it is necessary to camp in the place of regret at least temporarily. I would argue that camping in the place of regret could give clarity, focus, and direction regarding one's motivations. In other words, regret often forces a person to look into his or her heart and examine certain attitudes, fears, and the manner by which s/he makes sense of the world.

If there is an emotion we should let go of as quickly as possible, then it is guilt. Guilt stems from intentionally violating an accepted norm. Guilt has a paralyzing effect and keeps a person trapped in his or her past. Guilt feeds addiction, pain, and dysfunction, and corrodes every positive thing in one's life. When dealing with guilt, it is helpful to confront the past by owning up to the misdeed, and making an honest and earnest effort to change the behavior.

Conversely, regret is an emotion that often grows out of an unintentional action. Regret has a way of showing us how something can be done differently both today and in the future. Knowing the difference between regret and guilt is paramount to living a balanced and fulfilled life – a life free from self-blame and shame. I get it. We hate having regrets. Dealing with regrets makes us look unfocused, irresolute, error-prone, and weak. And who does not love displaying his or her strengths? We want to be seen as having it altogether.

We all wish we could get it right the first time. It is easy to look back at our past and see what we could have done better or differently. The reality is that no one gets it right the first time consistently. So, why not simply cut yourself some slack. It is perfectly fine to give yourself permission to pout and 'regret.' Really, it is.

We are developing beings through the lifespan and we get better with time. So, as it relates to regrets, no apologies are necessary.

Take Control of Your Personal Brand

The more I learn, the more I experience in life, the more I realize the necessity and value of being true to myself. Being true to myself grows out of self-belief, self-worth, and self-love, which means knowing my potential and abilities, NOT allowing myself to think negatively, and NOT allowing anyone to put me down.

Taking control of your personal brand begins by knowing who you are, what you stand for, and what you believe in. If you do not take control of your brand identity, then you are empowering others to create an unauthentic image and narrative of you. When you allow others to control your brand message, you are validating their flawed assumptions about you and allowing them to determine the value of your life and the outcomes you experience.

Yes, the way you think and act might challenge those around you. It might even offend some. If people have a problem with who you are— too bad! That is their problem, not yours.

Continually harness the power within and imprint your essence on the world's consciousness. Begin each day by taking control of your brand message. Be your own inspiration. Be powerful!

Difficult Does Not Mean Impossible

After 19 grueling days of twisting, stretching, lunging, swinging, dangling, and super-glued, sanded and bloody–tipped fingers, the painstaking journey of scaling one of the world's most difficult rock climb – the 3,000 feet wall of El Capitan in Yosemite National Park, culminated in success. Longtime friends Kevin Jorgeson and Tommy Caldwell became the first to successfully free-climb the world's biggest granite monolith.

This feat however, was not without its own set of unique challenges. In 2011, while attempting to scale the notoriously difficult Dawn Wall route, Jorgeson fell and broke his ankle, which sidelined him for an entire season. In 2013, Caldwell broke a rib when he inadvertently dropped a hundred-pound haul bag that was attached to his harness line. Prior to pulling off this remarkable endeavor, the duo had five unsuccessful attempts over a five-year span.

Before and during Jorgeson and Caldwell's attempt to free-climb the Dawn Wall, it was widely believed that the wall's steepness and lack of cracks and seams rendered it an improbable challenge. Even so, according to Jorgeson, "Climbing the Dawn Wall was not an effort to conquer; rather, it was about realizing a dream." Caldwell likewise viewed the climb as a "Spiritual experience more akin to something like 'painting' than extreme sports."

In an interview with ESPN, the interviewer asked Tommy (the more experienced climber of the two): "It's been about seven years in the making for you, why did climbing the Dawn Wall mean so much to you personally?" Tommy's response: "It was my way to explore the limits of what I thought were possible. It drove me everyday for seven years."

Every grueling pitch these men attempted was an opportunity to build muscle memory, increase physical endurance and strength, map the best routes, and develop better climbing techniques. The lesson here is that **difficult does not mean impossible** – something I'm learning every day.

Commit to the Grind

As part of her training to run her first full marathon, Meredith Fitzmaurice ran half-marathon races. At one of these events, namely the Run for Heroes Marathon, Meredith planned to do what she had successfully done at similar events—complete the half marathon route. Meredith and other runners lined up at the starting line and began this grueling race. At some point along the route, she glanced at her watch and wondered where the finish line was, as the run seemed longer than usual.

Moments later, Meredith realized that she had taken the "wrong" turn and was running the 26.2-mile full marathon route. In fairness to the other runners, she asked a bike marshal if her time would count toward the full marathon. The race official along with the race director determined that no rules were violated, thus giving Meredith the green light to continue the race. After 3 hours, 11 minutes, and 48 seconds, Meredith crossed the finish line in 10th place.

The story gets better. Meredith didn't simply cross the finish line. She won the women's race two minutes ahead of the second-place woman, capturing the women's title in the process. So what started out as a missed turn actually qualified Meredith to run one of the world's preeminent annual marathons–the Boston Marathon.

It was not a coincidence that Meredith won her race that day. Before Meredith laced her running shoes that morning, she had already determined her reality. Meredith's goal was to run a full marathon, and her reality became a reflection of what she did on a regular basis—**she committed herself to the grind!**

Are you committed to the grind?

Old-Fashioned Hard Work

The common denominator behind every success story and great accomplishment is...you guessed it, *hard work*. Not just any hard work, but the type of hard work that is tied to your life's passion. It is no secret that if you want to succeed at the highest levels and make your dreams become a reality, you need a solid work ethic.

Hard work is the *how* of success, meaning how you spend your time and resources working to accomplish your goals, and the hours you are spending each day developing your brand.

The interesting thing about the *how* of success is that it is not based on talent, skill, or background. That is, hard work tops talent every time. You can take the brightest person who's lazy, and put him against the hardest worker who might not be as talented, and the hard worker will prevail each time.

Do yourself a favor, and put in the time, hours, and work each day, and you'll become a great success. Remember, the way you spend your 24 hours today will determine whether or not you win tomorrow.

I Believe in Luck

There is a story of an old vigneron who used an advanced robot to work his vineyards. One day, the robot realized that it had the capacity to think and make its own decisions. After coming to this realization, the robot decided to leave the vineyard and explore the city. The neighboring vignerons sympathized with the old vigneron over his bad luck. The old vigneron said, "Is it bad luck or good luck? Who knows?"

A week later, the advanced robot returned with a group of less-advanced robots from the city, and the neighboring vignerons congratulated the old vigneron on his good luck. His reply was, "Good luck? Bad luck? Who knows?"

One day, as the less-advanced robots were harvesting grapes, they inadvertently damaged some vines. The neighboring vignerons thought that was bad luck. Not the old vigneron, whose only reaction was, "Bad luck? Good luck? Who knows?"

A few weeks later, swarms of aphids invaded the old vigneron's vineyards. But the noise generated by the less-advanced robots' mechanical parts incapacitated the aphids, saving the vineyard. Now, was that good luck or bad luck? Who knows?

The point of this story is that everything that seems on the surface to be bad luck may be good luck in disguise. And everything that seems to be good luck may be the opposite.

Nonetheless, what if luck is more than a series of random events that coincide with each other, yielding unintended or unplanned outcomes? What if luck is something that can be anticipated, even controlled?

What if luck is simply the result of anticipating and preparing for the opportunity of a lifetime?

Psychology Application

Mindset of Personal Success		
Concept	**Basic Premise**	**Theorist**
Fixed mindset	Assumes that our character, intelligence, and creative ability are static, which we can't change in any meaningful way.	Carol Dweck
Growth mindset	Thrives on challenge and sees failure not as evidence of unintelligence but as a heartening springboard for growth and for stretching our existing abilities.	
The Effort Effect	The effort effect is concerned with people's judgments about the causes of events and behavior. According to this theory, the key to success is to focus on growth, solving problems, and self-improvement.	

The Winner Effect		
Concept	**Basic Premise**	**Theorist**
The Winner Effect	The *winner effect* is a term used in biology to describe how an animal that has won a few fights against weak opponents is much more likely to win later bouts against stronger contenders. The winner effect also applies to humans in that success changes the chemistry of the brain, making one more focused, smarter, more confident, and more aggressive. People can work to improve their intelligence, thus improving their chances of winning. **What makes a winner?** Talent Confidence Practice Persisting through Failure Luck	Ian Roberson

Motivation and Achievement		
Concept	**Basic Premise**	**Theories/Theorists**
Motivation	Set of factors that activate, direct, and maintain behavior, usually toward some goal. **Views of motivation** An **intrinsic motivation** is a motivation to do an act for its own sake. An **extrinsic motivation** is based on the reinforcements and punishments that may follow an action. Most motivated behaviors result from a combination of intrinsic and extrinsic motivations.	Biopsychosocial theory of motivation Maslow's hierarchy of needs: interaction of biological, psychological, and social needs; lower motives (physiological and safety) must be met before higher needs (belonging, self-esteem).
Emotional Intelligence	Ability to know and manage one's emotions, empathize, and maintain satisfying relationships.	Peter Salovey and John D. Mayer

Motivation and Achievement (continued)		
Concept	**Basic Premise**	**Theorists**
Achievement Motivation	Referred to as the need for achievement, is an important determinant of aspiration, effort, and persistence when an individual expects his performance will be evaluated in relation to some standard of excellence.	J.W. Atkinson, & David McClelland
Performance-approach goal	is focused on attaining competence relative to others, a performance-avoidance goal is focused on avoiding incompetence relative to others.	
Performance-avoidance goal	is focused on avoiding incompetence relative to others.	
Mastery goal	is focused on the development of competence itself and of task mastery.	
Self-worth theory	Asserts that a person's ability to achieve is directly linked to his/her perceptions of him/herself.	Martin Covington

Part II: Career Success

What is career success? What does it look like? Would you be able to spot it if you saw it?

Does career success imply working for a fortune 100 company? Does it mean earning a huge salary with a massive golden parachute?

The reality is, if at this point in your life you have not defined what career success means to you, then someone else has already done it for you.

In other words, it is up to you to determine what career success looks like. While a job might be able to facilitate a successful career, a job in itself does not guarantee that you'll have a successful career. Having a successful career is entirely up to you.

So, how else could career success be defined? Career success, although different for everyone, occurs when your career direction aligns with who you are and what is important to you.[1]

In this section, success (i.e., winning) is about creating and exploring a world that enables you to find fulfillment. Winning is that awe-inspiring experience that comes from doing what you love.

---

[1] http://www.personalbrandingblog.com/10-essential-career-success-

Education Matters

$\mathbf{E}$ducation matters! There is no way around it. The fewer years of education you complete, the fewer opportunities that are open to you. The fact is, the more you learn, the more you earn.

Let's explore what education is <u>not</u>. Education does not mean going to college. There are many benefits of going to college; however, time spent in college is neither a measure of intelligence, nor fitness for a job, and it certainly does not guarantee career success.

Education is the discipline of discovering new possibilities, increasing knowledge and applying information in a manner that has practical value in the real world.

In a knowledge-based global economy, some type of formal education is a basic requirement for most jobs. For example, if a person is applying for an automotive mechanic position, the hiring organization will likely inquire about ASE certification.

The highest paid people are those who possess *intellectual capital*. This refers to people who know more of the critical facts, effective ideas, superior opportunities, and salient information than the average person in their field.

Formal education is highly correlated with higher income and occupational upgrading (i.e., promotions). So, while formal education does not guarantee career success, it most certainly increases your odds of winning.

College Is Not For Everyone

There is a myth that going to college somehow automatically improves one's life. Well, here is a dirty little secret about higher education. **All colleges and universities are for-profit businesses.** Colleges and universities are in the education business to make money, and they have gamed the system almost flawlessly—generating astronomical financial returns for stakeholders.

A college education; however, can open many doors of opportunities that might otherwise remain closed. Even so, the people with the loudest bullhorns, i.e., legislators, education lobbyists, university presidents, and financial institutions should stop propagating the myth and absurdity that going to college is the only gateway into the American middle-class and the only way to stay out of poverty.

Vocational, technical and digital education are other viable alternatives that have proven their worth in building economic growth. **Let's not forget about entrepreneurship.** One proven way to employment, financial security and self-fulfillment is to create a business. Don't believe me? Ask the following people, some of whom did not attend college and others who dropped out of college: Bill Gates, Paul Allen, Jennifer Aniston, Mark Wahlberg, Channing Tatum, Micky Arison, Jane Austen, Russell Simmons, Mark Zuckerberg, Ashley Simpson, Ted Turner, Will Smith, Naomi Campbell, James Cameron, Amanda Hocking, Michael Dell, Leighton Meester, Kate Moss, Steve Jobs, Larry Ellison, Oprah Winfrey, and the list goes on.

Every student has the right to a quality education; however, it has to be an education that is best suited for the individual. And sometimes the best education comes from the trial and error of pursuing one's passion and/or a once-in-a-lifetime opportunity.

An Entrepreneurial Mindset_The New Business Currency

We live in a society where economic structures and systems are designed to provide massive benefits to certain groups of people, while limiting access to other groups. The current system has limited well-paying opportunities and very few openings as it relates to reaching the top professionally.

Statistically, the odds are stacked incredibly high against some of us. The chance of achieving your career objectives, getting that corner office on the upper floor, earning above-market compensation and benefits—enough to buy your dream home, go on semi-annual vacations, fund your children's college education, take your spouse/partner to fine-dining restaurants, or enjoy the finer things in life, is slim.

Because of this, many people play it safe and lead lives far below their potential—spending the rest of their lives chasing the mechanical rabbit.

Despite those odds however, unparalleled success is within reach! BUT…to do so, in order to achieve your professional goals, you must change your strategic approach. The old model of learning a trade or getting a college degree is no longer the sure path to financial independence and security. That era is behind us.

If you want to command your own financial future, then you must adopt an **entrepreneurial mindset**, not a consumer mindset. An entrepreneurial mindset is committed to never-ending self-improvement. These individuals continually absorb inspiration and learn from and listen to success stories of people who inspire them to act and live their dreams and improve their lives and businesses.

Secondly, an entrepreneurial mindset looks for problems to solve. Thirdly, an entrepreneurial mindset produces and provides value to people's lives through the creation of useful products and/or services.

Here are four things entrepreneurs should keep in mind before launching a product and/or service.

1. **Is your product a consumable or durable good?**

   a. **Consumable goods** such as food, cosmetics, office supplies, toiletries, clothing, fuel and medicine tend to be stable; meaning, people tend to purchase these goods regardless of the economic environment. There is always money to be made with consumable goods. **Durable goods**, on the other hand, are items that do not have to be purchased frequently. These items include vehicles, jewelry, furniture, appliances, office equipment and consumer electronics.

   b. While there are opportunities to potentially earn great returns in the durable goods sector, the profit margin tends to be smaller.

2. **What problem does your product or service solve?**

    a. Uber made on-demand transportation more personal and efficient. Space X is on the way to making space travel more routine and affordable. Google made Internet search better. Scholly streamlined the process of finding college scholarships—they literally placed millions of dollars at students' fingertips. Airbnb made global vacation accommodations more convenient.

3. **Is your product an invention or innovation?**

    a. An invention is the creation of a unique product, service or process. An innovation, on the other hand, solves a pressing need. An innovation delivers an effective solution to a real problem people have.

4. **Is your product or service bridging the gap between what people are used to and what consumer trends are dictating?**

a. In essence, are you matching people with the best possible solutions to a recurring problem? Take for example, Under Armour. Founder, Kevin Plank—a former college football player disliked having to change out of his sweat-soaked t-shirts under his uniform. His teammates also hated that yucky feeling, and so did thousands of other collegiate and professional athletes. That was his opening. He identified the gap between what people were used to and what the market desired. After many days and nights of trial and error, he perfected a moisture-wicking synthetic fabric that kept athletes cool, dry and light.

Here's a practical exercise you can apply.

Get a sheet of paper, and draw a line down the middle. In the left column, write down at least three problems you would like to solve. For example, Problem #1 could be: *It is hard to locate my phone charger/cable at night, which sometimes causes my phone to die.*

<u>In the right column,</u> write down products/services that could address the problem(s) you listed in the left column. Here is a product that could address Problem #1: *A glow-in-the-dark phone charger/cable.*

After you have listed the problems and products/services, choose the one that appeals to you the most, and one with the greatest market potential—something you can easily monetized. Once you have completed the above steps, begin working on the following: (1) write a business plan; (2) choose a business structure; (3) assess your financing options; (4) get the proper licenses & registrations; (5) launch your company and make tons of money.

Too Stubborn To Fail

One common trait found among winners— those with sustained levels of winning, is stubbornness, i.e., tenacity, relentlessness and determination. **Winners are simply too stubborn to fail!** They neither allow "situationships" to darken their sunny days, nor allow people to dim their shine.

Winners are not overly concerned with failing as much as they are deliberate about winning. Here's how winners view failure:

1.   Winners understand that failure is not a person; therefore, they treat failure as a delay or interruption of a plan of action.

2.   Winners understand that failures are learning experiences, which is to say that failures demonstrate, often in a most striking fashion, alternative ways of winning.

3.   Winners know that failure is not an *end;* it is a *beginning*—an essential part of growth and success.

4.   Winners accept that failure does not hinder success; rather, failure gives them another opportunity to recast their vision and streamline the process of winning.

Over time, winners have learned to leverage failure. This is to say that winners tolerate failure, fail intelligently, learn from failure, reframe failure, and put failure to work.

Regard each failure as a necessary part and function of life. Allow each failure to tell you what you should or should not do as you move forward. The next time you experience *failure* be sure that you: (a) have learned a lesson; (b) will adapt to change; (c) will alter your plans; (d) change your thinking and behavior.

Success Is Not Easily Attained

Why won't you quit? Yes, you! I mean, life is coming at you at one hundred miles per hour, but still you choose to stand. Rather than throw in the towel, you salute life with the proverbial middle finger. So, what could possibly be worth it? The pursuit of happiness and the avoidance of pain…is that it?

It is the deepest desire for something greater. Success is what drives us to do the things we do. We all seek after success. Each of us, in one way or another, is trying to convert our skills and abilities into success (i.e., wealth). But why is it that only a small percentage of individuals actually become successful?

You see, while having a *no quitting* attitude is a great human quality, this quality by itself is not positively correlated with accumulating wealth.

Most people unwittingly live out their shadow selves (i.e., the dark and less favorable side of the personality) their entire lives because it never occurs to them that becoming wealthy is possible. And if living in abundance never occurs to them, then they never take any of the steps necessary to make becoming wealthy a reality.

So, change your mindset and understand this about success:

Success is not easily attained nor quickly conquered. She is elusive and love being pursued. She will recognize you if you acknowledge her irresistible power. She will give of herself to the degree of your commitment to study her, pursue her, cherish her and never let her go.

You Are Fired!

I read an article about an employee who wrote an <u>open letter</u> about her boss regarding her "<u>lousy pay</u>." Well, her action did not sit well with her boss, and she was promptly fired.

As with other issues, there were those who agreed with the boss' action, and there were those who sided with the employee.

Here's my position on this matter. If you put your job on blast, then you deserve to get your ass fired!

Here's my rationale. This employee's action speaks to a much bigger issue. There are so many employees who feel a sense of entitlement. Somehow, they believe that employers owe them something other than their paycheck just for being employed. They believe they should be first in line for a promotion or raise for which they have neither earned nor deserved. These employees add very little value to their place of employment; yet, demand that their employers reward them with CEO-level compensation and incentives.

This particular twenty-five-year old worker, in her open letter, complained about not being able to pay for her groceries, due in part to the exorbitant rent she was paying. Keep in mind that she moved to San Francisco knowing rent there was high. It gets better. Not only did she move to San Fran knowing that she could not afford the premium rent, she also started her life there with lots of personal debt. BUT here's the really interesting part. When she applied for that particular job, she knew what the job paid, and she agreed that the compensation and position were fair. Now all of a sudden, because she could not enjoy the lifestyle of a fairy princess, her problem became her boss' problem.

Really? Is this the way life works? You're not a producer. You're an avid and prolific and serial consumer. You're in debt to your eyeballs. You've made a series of poor choices with money, and you're still fiscally irresponsible. You're not a star player in your company. You are not a problem solver. You whine when you can't get your way. You feel a sense of entitlement because…uh…someone told you that you were special?

The problem isn't about your job not paying a living wage. The problem is that you think you are entitled to live like a prince or princess when you have the mindset of someone who is not interested in doing whatever it takes to win in life.

I am 100% in support of fair wages! And I am 100% against corporate greed. But I am also a proponent of earning…that is EARNING what you are worth. I am sorry, but you have not earned the right to demand $15, $17, or $20 an hour when your skill set clearly demonstrates that you're only worth $10 an hour.

So, what is the solution?

Quit making excuses. Find ways to increase your value. Make the necessary sacrifices to get what you're seeking after. And remember, good things come to those who wait, but greater things come to those who go after it!

Personal Branding

Personal branding is about aligning your vision, creative energy, desire to win, skill, and value, into a tangible, relevant, innovative, and practical, and useful product and/or service that change the way people live.

In order to leverage your brand, you must see yourself as a creator. First, begin with your name. That is, how do you perceive yourself, and how do others perceive you? What skills have you mastered, or presently mastering? What are your values and passions?

Second, what vehicle will you choose to make your brand available to others? For example, if helping people is your niche, then your vehicle might be a healthcare facility, working as a doctor, physical therapist, nurse anesthetist, or etcetera.

Third, what type(s) of product will represent your brand? Personally, some of the products that represent my brand are self-empowerment books, articles and blog posts about *Winning*. My products embody the values I represent and the awesome responsibility of making meaningful deposits in the lives of those within my sphere of influence.

It is important to note that your brand might not be limited to a specific industry or market. Here's an example. Although Steve Jobs' brand was heavily concentrated in the computing industry, he also branded himself in the music distribution business through iTunes. He founded the company, Pixar, which is responsible for creating awesome animated films such as Toy Story, The Incredibles (a personal favorite), Finding Nemo, Brave (another personal favorite), and others.

Thomas Peters puts it this way. "We are CEOs of our own companies: Me, Inc. To be in business today, our most important job is to be head marketer for the brand called You. [Personal branding] is that simple–and that difficult. And that inescapable."[2]

Remember, your brand will be the difference between a status-quo career and an exceptional career.

Ultimately, personal branding is making a

---

[2] http://www.fastcompany.com/28905/brand-called-you

full-time commitment to the journey of defining yourself as a leader and how this will shape the manner in which you will serve others.[3]

Networking

Building a successful career or business takes time. And since time is an invaluable commodity that should not be wasted, it necessitates finding efficient ways of taking your career or business to the next level.

A time-tested activity that is critical to your career and/or business success is networking. Networking is about building relationships. Effective networking produces long-term business-building results.

When done right, networking can raise your business profile and uncover new business opportunities. Strategic networking not only takes you to the right people, meaning, the people who are looking for new business, but also brings their business to you.

Networking is hard work, takes time, and might not yield immediate results. Even so, if you're truly serious about launching your brand, then consider how you are going to meet the needs of the larger community. Networking allows you to get an idea of how people might respond to your brand.

Remember, networking is not primarily about what you are going to get from a business relationship; rather, it is about what you have to offer others. Networking is about helping others to become successful—without an agenda.

Inevitably, when the business community perceives you as an asset, they will commit to the success of your brand. And the feedback you receive from networking will enable you to make the necessary adjustments to improve the overall quality and delivery of your products and services.

How to Dominate a Competitive Industry

In 1996, while sporting giants Nike and Adidas were busy trying to outduel each other—developing new sports technology innovations in an attempt to gain a competitive advantage, little did they know was that someone else was working triple duty in his grandmother's basement stitching various fabrics together to create the ultimate alternative to the cotton t-shirt. More than that, with this flagship product, this person had an ambitious plan to shake up the athletic apparel industry.

During that period, most of the major athletic shoes and apparel companies were focused on innovation relating to shoes and sporting equipment, and there was very little research and development done with apparel in mind. This was the opening this innovator was looking for. BUT rather than trying to dethrone Nike or the other major players, this new comer leveraged his ultimate hybrid t-shirt creation and began laying the foundation for his empire.

Going head-to-head with the big players was not going to be an easy task. First, those companies had stretched the limits of innovation and saturated the market with enough new and good products and services to last several years. Nonetheless, this pioneer understood that success was not to be measured by the abundance of good products and/or services one company or several companies put out in a given space.

He believed that even if the major players had rolled out a planet full of athletic shoes, sporting equipment and apparel, there was still enough room to make those products and services exponentially better. And with the foundation solidly laid, Kevin Plank launched Under Armour. In its first year, Under Armour made $17,000. Fast-forward twenty years—Under Armour now generates ~$4 billion in annual revenue.

So, how do you dominate a competitive industry? How do you upstage a dominant company? You don't. The interesting thing about life is that it always offers you an alternative strategy—one that ensures you come out on top.

Kevin Plank, a forward-thinking opportunist, struck the iron while it was hot; meaning, he capitalized on the opportunity to build, not a better sporting apparel, but the world's best sporting apparel.

Remember, there is at least one thing you can do better than anyone else. The key is finding out what that one thing is. Once you find out what *it* is, create *it*, market *it*, produce *it*, and give the world an opportunity to taste your creation and participate in your success.

The Kevin Durant Effect

There are several lessons that can be drawn from NBA player Kevin Durant's (KD) decision to leave the Oklahoma City Thunders for the Golden State Warriors. I will highlight two of those lessons.

First, it's okay to fire your boss—even if your boss is a decent human being. In the world of business, there is technically no such thing as employee or company loyalty. Your employer is impersonal and calculating, and is in the business of making money at your expense. You might be an accountant—perhaps the best accountant in your company, but don't ever confuse your title and/or position with your role. Your primary role is to ensure the continuous and stable distribution of profits to your company's shareholders. And once you are no longer considered a valuable company asset, you will be terminated, sacked, fired, let go, canned, dumped, discharged or made redundant.

This is not to say that it is impossible to win with the right employer. What I am saying is that to be totally dependent on any employer, hoping that the organization will support your long-term personal and professional aspirations and interests is a risk that should be considered carefully and wisely.

Second, loyalty is a both/and proposition. This suggests that not only is your employer in the business of profiting from your labor, but is also in the business of helping you win in life. Employer loyalty means that your organization should be as vested in your success as you are in theirs. Once more, loyalty is like a two-way street; therefore, if you plan to make demands of an employer, you'd better be worth your salt, which means:

- Always being on time.
- Serving with passion and integrity.
- Displaying an award-winning attitude.
- Treating co-workers and customers with respect and dignity.

- Fulfilling your duties and responsibilities with scrupulous care, diligence and efficiency—as if you owned the company.

Finally, in business, the best kind of loyalty is when both parties, i.e., the employer and employee, are benefiting. Whatever your position, whether as an employee or entrepreneur, your job should give you the freedom and opportunity to expand your intellectual capacity, make mistakes, be a better decision-maker, build character and become a better person.

Psychology Application

Career Success Mental Models		
Concept	**Basic Premise**	**Theorists**
Systems Thinking	Systems thinking is a way of looking at the world that allows you to see how many small pieces come together to make a more complex whole. Moving from simple to highly complex tasks in stages.	• Ludwig von Bertalanffy • W. Ross Ashby • Peter Senge
Personal power	Personal power is one's capacity to realize one's personal purpose. People only begin to fulfill their creative potential when they have a high degree of personal alignment in their lives. That is, when their pursuits and conscious goals, the things they are	

	actually committed to, are in line with their own personal purpose.	

Part III: Financial Success

What is financial success? How do we measure it? And what does it look like? Does financial success mean having the spending power to change market trends? Or is it about being able to live comfortably and reinvesting in one's own future?

Perhaps, financial success means living within one's means and avoiding consumer debt. What if financial success is simply a tool for doing more—a tool for expanding one's portfolio so as to change one's family tree for generations?

It is no secret that financial prudence is the key to building wealth. A person does not need a high degree of social competence or the highest IQ to become financially successful. A person who desires financial security however needs to be willing to make sacrifices upfront and wise investment choices in order to convert small financial opportunities into long-term winning financial opportunities.

Some say that wealth building is 90% behavior and 10% knowledge. Others maintain that financial success is an intentional and driven mindset. Well, let's explore together.

Wealthy Mindset

In order to become wealthy, you must change the way you think about money. You must treat money like a living thing.

When it comes to making money, *you* are the primary generator of income, not your job. You are the boss, and each morning you get up, you are selling your brand, or your labor.

Think of it this way. Each dollar is an operative (an employee) in your business. Each dollar should have the same goal as you do, and that is to make enough money to earn more money.

So, before you hand over that dollar, ask yourself, how much profit is that dollar going to bring in. If you must, give each dollar a name. No kidding.

Once you get to the point where each dollar is bringing in more dollars, then *you* no longer have to sell your labor. Your goods and services, which are now an extension of your labor, will automatically generate wealth for you.

At the end of the day, remember, cash is king, and being wealthy is a good thing.

Start with a Budget

The all-important first step in creating wealth starts with having a budget. Most millionaires will tell you that systematic budgeting played a key role in them becoming millionaires.

Here are three items to consider when creating a budget. First, determine how much income you have. Second, estimate all of your expenses. And third, subtract the expense total from the income. A negative number means that you have to return that expensive diamond ring you bought for your wife. Okay, I'm just kidding.

A negative number actually means that you're living above your means. Basically, you're spending too much. A positive number suggests that you're headed in the right direction.

Here's the deal folks. Budgeting is an adult decision to win with money. Budgeting helps stop the cash leakage, and puts you in control of your life.

Budgeting is not primarily about crunching numbers. Budgeting is a way of life, because winning is a way of life.

Refer to the budget worksheet at the end of the book.

Spend Less Than You Earn

There is a cascade of positive effects that come from spending less than you earn. First, it's simple math, and it just makes sense. Second, spending less than you earn is a great way to attack and eliminate debt (including your home mortgage and student loans). Third, spending less than you earn enables you to pile plenty of cash into a savings account, which comes in handy especially when Murphy[4] decides to show up. Believe me, he WILL show up. The question is, will you be ready?

If a swimming pool looses more water than it retains, you might not want to jump off the diving board, or you could be seriously injured. The same principle can be applied to our discussion. Spending more than you earn is a sure way to insolvency,

---

[4] Anything that can go wrong, will go wrong.

stress, stress and more stress.

Finally, spending less than you earn helps you gain financial momentum, which is essential to building tremendous wealth. Spend less, save more, and live well. You'll be happier for it.

Save, Save, Save

I was a nineteen-year-old college student, single, working, living the life, and enjoying a really nice two-bedroom apartment. There was one problem, however. For a reason that was not obvious then, I struggled to pay my rent.

Even so, I never panicked because I had the best insurance plan a nineteen year old could have—my dad. Well, one day, my *insurance plan* got canceled.

It was a routine phone call (so I thought). "Hey dad, how's it going? … Things are a bit tight, and…uh…can you help me out this month with my rent." Dad speaking: "Hi son, I'm glad you're doing well. Let me ask you, how much do you make? And give me a breakdown of all your expenditures."

The conversation ended with my dad telling me that the problem I faced was not an income problem, but a responsibility problem. He said, "If you earn, then spend without a savings plan, you will be back to square one, which is being broke."

Solution:

1. Pay yourself first.
2. Build an emergency fund that can cover at least six months of expenses.
3. Invest.
4. And avoid debt as you would the bubonic plague.

Avoiding Debt

Debt is a destabilizing force that exponentially increases risk and the probability of fatal failure.[5]

Although debt is something you should avoid like the bubonic plague, many people believe that debt is a prerequisite to wealth-building. That belief is absolutely asinine, entirely misguided, fashionably speculative and mired in utter ignorance and blinding stupidity.

One of the keys to wealth-building is to avoid debt. And if you do assume temporary debt, let it be toward something that generally increases in value, like a real estate. Another exception for assuming debt is purchasing a home. Even then, pay down 20% in cash, and assume no more than a 15-year fixed rate mortgage for the balance.

Each time you borrow, you are in essence

[5] Ramsey, D. (2011). EntreLeadership. New York, NY: Howard Books.

making yourself a slave to the lender. The master (i.e., lender) has total and absolute discretion over the funds and the high-status artifacts (e.g., car, house) that were purchased with the borrowed funds.

Enjoy financial freedom by avoiding debt.

Wage Slave or Employee?

Are you an employee or a wage slave? Oh…you have not heard of the term "wage slave?"

A wage slave or <u>wage slavery</u> refers to a situation where a person's livelihood depends on wages or a salary. Based on statistical analysis of employment data, I can say with a degree of certainty that over 90% of those reading this chapter fall under the "wage slave" category. I know—*slave* is such a bad word, and no one want's to admit to being a slave. But the sooner you realize and acknowledge your true condition, as a wage slave, the quicker you can change your circumstances.

Before you start beating yourself up, keep in mind that it is most likely NOT your fault that you are a wage slave. It's likely that most of you were not born into a wealthy family, and you still have not won the lottery. Chances are, you are a product of many generations of regular folks who got up and did the eight-to-five for thirty years—worked, retired, then died. That's the past though. So, how do we change that narrative?

The first step to changing the corporate slave narrative is to **KNOW YOUR VALUE**. You have to accept once and for all that YOU ARE SPECIAL. I know this reads like cliché, but if you do not assign a value to your life, you'd better believe that some employer that does not have your best interest at heart will attach a value to you.

The second step to changing the corporate slave narrative is to **WORK ON YOUR WORK**. Seriously...I'm so sick and tired of listening to the noise and chatter about dreams, planning, goal-setting, visioning, hoping and praying. You can do those things until you pass out. It is not until you *work on your work* that you will be able to escape the corporate plantation to freedom.

If you want to write for a living, then you must get the ball rolling by writing everyday. If your goal is to start your own business, which is the premise of this chapter, then you should take the following steps.[6]

---

[6] Retrieved from http://www.businessnewsdaily.com/4686-how-to-start-a-business.html

The reality is, too often, the place where you work is simply a business—a cold and thankless merchant of greed making money at your expense. While you're busy busting your butt on the night shift, do you know where your boss is? He is in bed watching Netflix or sound asleep. When you are forced to go to work on your off days, or on days you're not feeling well, do you know what your boss is doing? She is probably vacationing in Milan, Italy with her friends and family.

Some of you might be tempted to boast about your handsome compensation package and how well your company treats you. Well, you might want to temper your celebration. Because it really does not matter whether you work for a mom-and-pop operation or a fortune 100 company. Working a job is like paying rent. You may have a nice place but it's not yours.

You can no longer afford to waste your precious days living from paycheck-to-paycheck, barely getting by and not knowing how you're going to take care of your family.

The prospect of spending the rest of your life working an eight-to-five job should terrify you.

Life is short, and the time to pursue your dreams is NOW. The truth is, there is not anything more rewarding than being in a job you love—a job you created.

Remember, life is not a rehearsal. There is no backup feature, delete function, reverse option or second chance. You only get one chance, one opportunity to live your life with purpose, so don't waste it.

Trust and act like you are one ingredient, one step, and one action away from experiencing the life you've always imagined. Trust yourself, trust the process, and make the sacrifices today so that you can live like no one else tomorrow.

Start Your Own Business

According to research[7], starting your own business is the most effective and proven way to build tremendous wealth. Studies have found that entrepreneurs are four times more likely to become millionaires than those who work for others.

Keep in mind that entrepreneurship is not for persons with an average mindset. Entrepreneurship, ladies and gentlemen, is for individuals with stick-to-itiveness. Because of the cost factor and time commitment involved, starting your own business is something you should not take lightly. Starting your own business will test your grit and resolve.

There will be times when you will have to put sleep on hold until you finish a project. There will be other times when you will have to cancel

---

[7] Stanley, T.J., Danko, W.D. (2010). *The Millionaire Next Door.* Amazon Digital Services, Inc.

that dinner reservation, or postpone that vacation.

Even so, the rewards are huge for those who are able to start and operate a profitable business.

Choosing the Right Career Path

Imagine waking up one day only to realize that your marriage was a complete and absolute mistake. The person whom you married turned out to be the worst thing to have ever happened to you.

Now, let's imagine waking up one day only to realize that your career is completely off course, meaning, going to work saps your energy, gives you homicidal ideation, and makes your life depressingly miserable.

Okay, I admit that choosing a career path is not exactly like choosing a spouse. The point is, choosing the right career path does not have to be an anxiety-filled experience that causes a lifetime of unremitting stress.

Choosing the right career path should be evaluated alongside your *present* skills, values, and motivation, not future ambition. [To find out your dominant motivation focus as it relates to your personal and professional life, visit http://www.yourfocusdiagnostic.com/].

The right career path: (1) provides you with opportunities to learn and grow; (2) adds value and meaning to other areas of your life; (3) pays extremely well.

I have a friend who earns a six-figure salary working nine months out of the year. This person spends the remaining three months pursuing varied interests, such as traveling, thrill and adventure seeking, blogging, and volunteering.

Here's what he shared with me. "Ultimately, choosing the right career path should be based on doing what comes natural to you, and doing what you enjoy most."

Laughing to the Bank

The first 24 hours of the 2016 National Basketball Association (NBA) free agency period was marked by contracts so huge that it would make your head spin—we're talking about eight and nine-digit multimillion dollar contracts.

Last year, the typical <u>American earned $44,569</u>, and that was before taxes. During the same period, <u>LeBron James earned $22,970,500</u>. And this does not include his endorsement deals. To put this in context, @ $44,569, it would take the average American 515 years to make what LeBron James earned (NBA salary) in one year.

In a society where salaries and wages have remained stagnant for decades, do professional athletes really get paid too much money? Absolutely not!

We live in a free market society/economy, where each person has the freedom to pursue his or her dreams—unencumbered by limitations of ethnicity, gender, religion, sexuality or disability. I find it absolutely detestable how obsessed people are regarding other people's money and what other people have. I mean, seriously, if you are sitting around and are more concerned about how much someone else makes for a living, you are a pitiful person!

I would say to all those complaining, rather than complain and publicly display your jealousy and envy, why not evaluate your own skills and talents and prove to everyone how market worthy your skills really are. I mean, you think so highly of yourself—so, show everyone what you are really worth.

The fact is: the law of supply and demand makes it possible for athletes to earn the big bucks. Here's another fact: YOU have all the freedom in the world to pursue your millions, even billions. So, quit being a wuss and stop worrying about what other people have or how they live.

So, to those who complain about athletes being overpaid: Professional sports leagues generate revenue because fans pay to watch. You got a problem with athletes being overpaid? Turn off the television. Don't go to games. Don't buy the gear. Otherwise, stop complaining!

Putting It All Together

Achieving financial success is not as difficult as you might imagine. It is like cleaning and maintaining a swimming pool.

I remember sharing in the excitement with my family after we secured a house with a pool. I thought of the pool parties my children would get to enjoy from the comfort of their own backyard.

The time came to get the pool ready for the summer. With my supreme confidence in one hand, and pool supplies in the other, I began preparing the pool. On day one, I raked the bottom of the pool and removed as many leaves and debris as possible. Day two, I shocked the water. By day three, the water was starting to turn, but remained cloudy.

Day eleven came and the water was still cloudy, and I was ready to quit. That was until I came across a blogger who offered the following advice. He said, "Repeat after me: 'Shock, run filter, brush, vacuum. Shock, run filter, brush, vacuum.'" I thought, "what the heck." I implemented the steps, and to my surprise, it worked.

So, do you want to achieve financial success? Then repeat after me: "Make money, pay yourself, spend less than you earn, invest, avoid debt, repeat."

Psychology Application

Behavioral Finance		
Concept	**Basic Premise**	**Theorist**
Behavioral Finance	Understanding behavioral finance is important. Because of it we are aware of our tendencies, and we can set up our financial life to take these tendencies into account. If we pretend that financial mismanagement does not exist then we will continue to act in a way that is financially self-defeating.	Retrieved from http://www.vakkur.com/hx/beh_fin_sum.htm
Heuristics	Heuristics—the process by which people find things out for themselves, usually by trial and error.	
Mental accounting	Mental accounting is the set of cognitive operations used by individuals and households to organize, evaluate, and keep track of financial activities.	Richard Thaler

Behavioral Finance		
Concept	**Basic Premise**	**Theorist**
Emotion	Human emotion involves physiological arousal, expressive behaviors, and conscious experience. Emotions play a critical role in how individuals behave and react to external stimuli; Emotions and mood can cloud judgment and reduce rationality in decision-making.	Source: Myers, D. (2011). *Exploring Psychology.* New York, NY: Worth Publishers.
Regret	Regret—the emotion experienced for not having made the right decision. Regret is more than the pain of loss. It is the pain associated with feeling responsible for the loss.	
Self-attribution Bias	People attribute successful outcomes to their own skill but blame unsuccessful outcomes on bad luck. Having a financial adviser enables the investor to carry out a shifting of responsibility if things go wrong.	Fritz Heider

Part IV: Relational Success

Relational intimacy. What is it? And how is it achieved?

Out of the myriad factors connected to relational intimacy, I have chosen to highlight the factors I believe that are most germane to contemporary relationships. My rationale for this approach is based on the following.

This is the first time in history where relationships are no longer mutually exclusive to a certain worldview, ideology, value system or traditional family structures. The dawn of the 21st century has introduced an infinite array of unimagined possibilities, which make traditional assumptions about contemporary relationships obsolete.

The balance of power has equalized in that men are no longer the only *breadwinners* in the home. In fact, in many households, the woman earns much more than her spouse. In some cases, men are building their careers from the home, which enables them to care for their children while providing an opportunity for their spouses to lead multinational corporations. It is evident that the dynamics of relationship between men and women have undergone a sea of change compared to that in the past.

With this new shift, it would seem quite logical that a different and new approach for examining relationships is warranted. Well, it depends on how deeply you choose to examine the contemporary relationships.

From a birds-eye perspective it appears that contemporary human relations have evolved as quickly as technology has. However, if you were to look closely, you would notice that some of the same relational dynamics that existed before the 21st century are still present today.

I invite you to join me on this quest to determine whether our assumptions about relational intimacy correspond with the *new* way we view the world.

Dirty Laundry

Let's start by defining the words "Dirty Laundry." In the literal sense, dirty laundry refers to soiled and unclean articles of clothing. Within the context of this chapter, dirty laundry refers to the baggage a person brings into a relationship.

There are several levels of dirty laundry. Most often, dirty laundry is easily washed, and is reusable. Next, there is the dirty laundry that is so filthy that in order to get it cleaned well, the washer has to be set on the heavy-duty, hot water, high agitation, extra rinse, and high spin cycle, with heavy duty laundry detergent and bleach added. Then, there is the dirty laundry with stains that have sat for so long, and are so deep that the dirty laundry is unsalvageable and has to be discarded.

On a superficial level, each person brings

some baggage into a relationship. Those things might be simple, yet annoying habits such as cursing, burping, flatulence (passing gas), loud chewing, loud and obnoxious behavior in public, poor listening skills (interrupts you every two sentences). While those habits might be considered romantic wrecking balls, they are somewhat washable (fixable).

The next level of dirty laundry is the filthy articles of clothing that have to be washed in hot water and bleach in order to remove the stains and get the clothes cleaned properly. As it relates to relationships, these habits might include smoking, drinking, overeating, undereating, spending in excess of one's income, fault finding, uncompromisingly lazy, easily irritated, and self-centered. While these habits can ruin any relationship, they can be fixed with the right amount of support, encouragement, and counseling.

The next level of dirty laundry is the dirty laundry that is near unsalvageable. In the relationship context, these habits and behaviors not only destroy the relationship, but also demoralize the person in the process. These habits include, physical and emotional abuse, serial infidelity, dishonesty, unforgiveness, constant comparing to others, and /or criminal activity.

The essence of this chapter centers on transparency. I decided to begin this section with a chapter on trust because trust is the foundation of lasting relationships.

For those of you in relationships, you owe it to each other to be upfront about your dirty laundry. Of course, there are certain things you might not be aware of until someone brings it to your attention. For example, the mustard or ketchup stain on your shirt or blouse. But those are not the dirty laundry I am referring to. I am talking about the part of self— the limitations you are keenly aware of, and might still be addressing.

The point is, it is better to be upfront *now* about a certain experience, issue, or limitation you might have had or still have, than to wait until the evening of the honeymoon to confess your secret.

There's an account of a guy who successfully sued his wife for damages caused by their divorce. The story is, after this couple got married, they had a child. The man could not understand how their child could be so ugly considering that he was average looking, and his wife was, by cultural account, a beautiful woman.

Subsequent investigation revealed that the

mother of the child had cosmetic surgery, which made her more physically appealing. The wife withheld that fact from her husband.

Once trust is compromised or broken, it's like Humpty Dumpty—hard to put back together. Furthermore, unresolved issues tied to your past and present might inevitably create an inherently insecure, unhappy and unfulfilled relationship.

Men, don't wait until after the wedding night to let your wife know that you spent your early years sowing your royal oats, and your paycheck might be a little short on funds because of child support. Be upfront in your relationship early on, and accept responsibility for your past actions.

Give your woman the opportunity to make a decision as to whether she wants to take a role in rearing your child(ren). In other words, come clean. If you still have a substance abuse proclivity or any other habit that could minimize the integrity of the relationship, you certainly need to make your lady aware.

Leave no stone unturned as it relates to your struggles and limitations. Being transparent means that your partner might be willing to help you shore up your limitations. Or s/he might decide that helping you is not worth the investment.

Even so, it is best to let your significant other decide for him or herself if he or she wants to remain in the relationship while the kinks or dysfunctions in your life are being worked out. To withhold a known limitation from your companion is deceitful, and will lead to manipulative practices in the relationship.

Ladies, the same goes for you. You should be honest with your man early on. If you are living with a certain fear, then by all means, inform your mate. If the emotional scars of past relationships are still visible in your mind, it might be helpful and even therapeutic to let your partner know that.

Here's the heart of the matter. Your history is a part of your present life. Your experiences made you the person you are today.

Consider this: If you don't share your dirty laundry, the question becomes, what other secrets would you be willing to hide from your partner. Have you truly divested yourself of your previous relationship baggage?

Here's a real life account that was shared with me by a reader, whose permission I received to share her story.

* * *

"Josiah, I did just that...exactly as you mentioned...I had children from previous relationships, and was not always the upright woman that I am today. I met a man whom I thought was a fabulous person.

Before taking our relationship to the next level, I believe it was best to be upfront about issues with which I still struggled. Well, for the first few months of our marriage, it appeared like everything was going well. Then my husband began asking more and more deeply personal questions about my past.

For example, he wanted me to compare my previous sexual relationships with his performance. And I refused to go along. He became demanding, and started digging for more information. I resisted because I was upfront with him about everything he needed to know.

Well, he became very controlling and the relationship quickly deteriorated. He started monitoring my every move. He would show up to my job unannounced and mask his action by presenting me with flowers.

When my husband saw me talking to another guy, he would ask, 'What did he want?

Why were you smiling like that? Did you give him your number? What were y'all talking about?'

I became increasingly uncomfortable, and I told him that his actions were not becoming of a man whom I had learned to trust, love, and forgive. I could share details of my ex-husband's less than stellar moments, but that's beside the point.

Unfortunately, the beginning of the end of our relationship occurred when my ex-husband became physically abusive. He never hit me, but on several occasions he shoved me, squeezed my arms tightly, and physically cornered me when he couldn't get his way, or until he was satisfied with the response I gave him.

The relationship actually ended when I found out he was having an affair with my best friend. They had been fooling around for almost two years before I found out.

If that's what you're suggesting when you say *transparency* then good luck—because I'm not going down that path again."

* * *

I can't begin to imagine the hurt and emotional toll this precious woman went through, and perhaps is still going through. Her story is a story of ultimate betrayal, and one that's all too common.

The reality is that this relationship did not end because of transparency issues. The relationship ended because of abuse, duplicity, selfishness and unfaithfulness. That is, her ex-husband's own insecurities, pretension, and double standard destroyed their promising relationship.

Yes, there are risks associated with transparency and giving someone your heart. There is also learning / growing in the risking.

If trust and transparency are qualities your partner is lacking, then perhaps s/he is not someone that should be a part of your life.

Some individuals believe that certain experiences about one's life are best left in the past. And I support this position. Whatever path you choose, be sure that it is a decision that both you and your companion are willing to live with.

Each person comes into a relationship with some dirty laundry. Some enter with dirty laundry that is easily cleaned. Others enter into a relationship with laundry that is so soiled that the relationship fails before it even begins.

Each person, at one time or another has

fallen off life's wagon, meaning, making regrettable decisions. It takes tremendous courage to admit one's failings and imperfections.

Your honesty is not evidence of weakness. Conversely, your honesty shows that you are a person of character.

Man Up

Men, dudes, bruhs, fellas…this section is just for you. Has anyone given you the 411 on your life's assignment and your reason for being a man? Do you know what your primary responsibilities are, as the foremost dominant male of all male species in the universe? Well, you're about to find out.

Men, your first responsibility is to take care and maintain the earth. No, I'm not living in a tree house on a hill, drinking spring water, bird watching, and sun gazing. I live in the suburbs like most of you. I have a family, a business, and tons of other responsibilities.

By taking care and maintaining the earth, I am referring to being an agent of change. Here's what I'm asking: Are you engaged in meaningful work? In what ways are the fruits of your effort and labor promoting and advancing solutions relating to social consciousness, social progression and liberty? Does your reason for living revolve around making other people's lives better?

Your second responsibility as a man is to work. By work, I am not talking about playing the latest video games, or binge television watching. I am referring to forty to sixty hours per week, grinding in the area of your expertise.

I find it very difficult to sympathize with men who complain about how tough life is, and how difficult it is to get ahead. Listen fellas, if you really want to get ahead in life, get a job! Get two jobs, maybe three. And you'll get to your intended destination.

Your third responsibility as a man is to serve your family. Serving your family means protecting, nurturing and educating.

Men, in order to protect, nurture, and educate your family, you must be present. You cannot give anything of substance to your family if you are not an active part of their lives. Be there for your son, and model to him how to be a real man. The same consideration should be given to your daughter. She needs you in her life even as your son does.

The *education* aspect of this responsibility

means to share your life experiences with your family. For example, if you had a challenging day at work, plan a family meeting and share with your family the problem-solving strategies you utilized to deal with a difficult assignment, team member or boss.

Nurturing refers to empowering your family. This involves sharing in household chores and responsibilities, establishing rules and limits, encouraging communication, and creating routine and structure. Nurturing also involves listening to your lady and children. Be deliberate in planning the amount of quality time you are going to spend which each member of the household.

Men, to protect your family means to fight with them in combating cultural influences, making sound and healthy entertainment choices that the whole family could learn from and enjoy, or talking to your children about the risks of social media, and so forth.

Sir, your woman also needs your protection, but not the protection that involves a shootout with your neighbor. I am simply referring to satisfying her emotional, mental, sexual and spiritual needs.

Here's the essence of manhood. A MAN takes care of his family. A MAN makes decisions that put his family on a winning trajectory. A MAN neither makes excuses, nor lounges around idly or without specific purpose. A MAN leaves the cave and returns only after he makes a kill large enough to support his family. A MAN digs in, grinds, goes all in—in the pursuit of his dreams, goals and aspirations. A MAN encourages his woman to pursue her highest ambitions. A MAN might disagree with his woman, but will never, ever, resort to physical or emotional abuse. A MAN admits when he is wrong, and apologizes even when he is in the right. A MAN not only nurtures his children, but also challenges them to stretch beyond the limits of their creative endurance. A MAN respects and cares for the natural environment. A MAN embraces his spiritual identity and oneness with the universe.

Woman Up

Women, ladies, sisters—YOU are an elegantly fascinating beautiful and intellectual person. And there is no one else on earth like you!

I believe that about you because I have great admiration for women and understand how women think.

Considering that I was born of a woman. I am married to a woman. And I have been raising three beautiful women who share my DNA. I believe these realities qualify me to share what I have learned about women.

Ladies, if you're trying to multitask while reading this chapter, I ask your permission to pause for a moment, as what I am about to share with you will have practical implications in your everyday experiences with other people; particularly, men.

Ladies, has anyone given you the scoop on your life's assignment and your reason for being a woman? Do you know what your primary responsibilities are, as the foremost dominant female of all female species in the universe? Well, you're about to find out.

Women, your first responsibility is to live your life as a whole person. In other words, when/if you decide to share the essence of who you are with another person, you're not entering into the relationship to be complete. No, no! When you choose to share the essence of your being, you are simply giving that person the opportunity of a lifetime—an opportunity to participate in your completeness.

Take a moment to reflect on that gem.

Your second responsibility as a woman is to regulate your environment. Your power to influence is one of the strongest forces in the universe. The universe bends to the will of a woman who is aware of her identity and essence. There isn't any obstacle, impediment, barrier, difficulty, hardship, handicap, obstruction, restriction, hurdle, hitch, wall or mountain that can get in the way of a woman who lives and experiences the highest fulfillment of self.

Women, your third responsibility is to express your femininity—without apology. The sphere in which you can express your femininity is all-encompassing as eternity itself. Your birthright–your femininity, is specifically purposed to sustain the planet, your mate, and your children.

It is the overarching acceptance of your femininity that instills in others the gifts of beauty, graciousness, self-efficacy, self-concept, strength, confidence, gentleness, happiness and joy.

The gift of your femininity inspires love, forgiveness, faith, hope, courage, resolve, longsuffering, compassion, trust, selflessness, peace and sacrifice.

Your femininity is an enduring strength that continually shines throughout history, time and space. Your femininity is a gift of the universe's creative intelligence.

Mate-Retention Strategy

Men, here are two things women find most unattractive about you.

There isn't anything about *laziness* that impresses a woman. Hard work that is tied to your passion is impressive.

I'm not going to belabor this point other than saying that an honorable man is a man with a vision and practical plan for winning. A man who is worthy of a great woman is a man of sound character and judgment. And a man with a job–not just any job, but a good paying job.

Ladies, if you're dating a guy who makes excuses as to why he is unemployed, underemployed, or sporadically employed, I can tell you now—you have trouble on your hands. Ladies, if any man shows little interest in holding a job, he is not worth your time, energy and investment.

The second thing women find most

unattractive about men is: a guy who embraces *average*. Here's what an average guy thinks and acts like.

Men with an average mentality believe that women are not their equals. These men believe that a woman's place should be reduced to being pregnant and bare feet in the kitchen. These men do not help out with household chores. They do not unload the groceries or wash dishes. They believe that some work was designed strictly for women.

An average guy is satisfied with life as it is. This is a man who is neither interested in refining his strengths, nor developing his limitations. This man is happy working an 8-5 job, then coming home to spend the remaining hours glued to the television set, or playing video games. And you'd better not disturb him. Of course, he wouldn't mind you bringing him his meal and some lemonade.

The average man is one who does not treat his lady with the respect she deserves. Ladies, do not embrace any relationship where you're treated like an object, or reduced to playing second fiddle.

Men, you're born to be great and achieve unparalleled success. Embrace your destiny, and start believing and living like the great man you are. Your woman will appreciate you so much more. If you do not claim your birthright, do not be surprise if she passes you up for someone who is living in the essence of his manhood—greatness.

The Gold Fish
Mentality

Ladies, here are two things men find most unattractive about women.

#1. A woman who has to be constantly reminded about her intrinsic worth and physical beauty.

Women, if you need a man to validate you, then *you need a checkup from the neck up.* I understand we live in a society that glamorizes certain aspects of what constitutes beauty, while ignoring what truly matters; like, character, attitude, depth, resolve and authenticity.

Mainstream media along with the entertainment industry have popularized the notion that a beautiful and complete woman is a socialite, light-skinned, waffle-thin, clueless, liberated, inarticulate, loves to shop, obsessed with penis size, wears sleazy clothing, fixated with cosmetic surgery, vain, dippy and common.

Ladies, you are so much more than society's definition of you. A truly beautiful woman is more than just eye candy. In men's eyes, a truly beautiful woman is a complete woman who dons her *completeness*—one who is self-secure, has positive self-concept, high self-efficacy, graceful, unpretentiousness, charismatic and classy.

–Men prefer substance over flash. –

#2. Ladies, please, please, please: (1) stop acting desperate; (2) And stop giving up your heart and body so easily. I know he got the juice. I realize he's finer than red wine. I understand that he's chiseled and physically endowed like a Greek god. And I know you desire him. But respect yourself enough to let the *right* person into your life.

Your eagerness to find a man should not be reduced to sleeping with every player who whispers sweet nothings in your ears. Desperation is unattractive. And the last thing a man wants on his hands is a thirsty woman.

For the record, just because men find certain things unattractive about you does not mean they will not attempt to sleep with you. If you're that easy, then it's not his fault.

Here's the point, ladies. The less certain you are of your identity as a woman of promise and honor, the easier it will be for you to compromise your values and minimize the gift of your femininity.

Ladies, if a man perceives you as someone who is at peace being single; someone who is composed in the midst of sexual desire; and someone who is unruffled by others' opinions, then he sees you as a winner and someone worth getting to know.

Here's another perspective.

Women, as it relates to finding the right mate, you will most likely get what you're looking for. You will attract what you are. If your expectations are low, then you'll end up with a joker, a shell of a man—a loser.

For the women who say, "The pickings are slim" or "All the good men are taken," that is simply not true. Once again, you will find what you're looking for.

If you want a luxury vehicle, then you can't go car shopping on a Chevy, Ford, Honda, or Toyota dealership lot. You're going to have to visit a Maserati or Bugatti showroom.

Likewise, relational success will not occur by osmosis or vicariously. Relational success— finding that right person is the result of looking in the right direction and wise decision-making.

When a woman buys into the myth that there aren't any good men available, do you know what she is more than likely to do? She will lower her standards, compromise her values, and settle for the next best loser that comes along.

Women, the good man whom you desire will not walk into your arms if your mentality and lifestyle suggest that you are not ready to receive such a man. If you're preoccupied trying to get it together, the *good man* will likely pass you by to find a woman who is basking in the rays of her completeness.

Ladies, I know this is a hard truth to swallow, but it is a necessary truth to share. As it relates to finding the right man, begin by asking yourself, "What do *I* bring to the table? And how can I improve my stock?

You can start by loving yourself, not the way you think a man should love you, but in truth, fullness and positive self-affirmation. If you center your existence on self-love, grace, passion, strength, and industry, then you will eventually attract a good man—the right man for you.

Tabula Rasa

The one common and unavoidable variable that exists in every relationship is conflict. It is inevitable that you and your significant other will have disagreements. Even so, the manner by which you agree to disagree will lead to either the strengthening or weakening of your relational bond.

When managed civilly and in consideration of each other's best interests, conflict can serve as a catalyst for acceptance and an opportunity for long-term healthy relational intimacy. Here are a few steps for addressing and resolving conflicts.

Step one is to **listen.** When you take time to listen, problem solving ensues and conflicts are resolved without causing unnecessary duress to the relationship. **Being a listening presence is a gift of love.** Being a listening presence validates a person's personhood, and gives permission to the individual to experience wholeness and aliveness.

Step two in settling relational conflict is to **acknowledge the ways you might have contributed to the conflict**. Admit you were wrong. Owning up to your mistakes puts your partner at ease, and invites civility and honesty into the conversation.

Step three is to **apologize for not catching the problem before the problem got out of control**. Assure your mate that you'll be more proactive as it relates to monitoring your own behavior, and will be more in tuned to his/her needs.

The final step is to **wipe the slate clean** (i.e., tabula rasa). This means you will point out the problem the first time it occurs, and once the conflict is resolved, you will never bring up the issue again.

$ Bling Bling $

A widely propagated myth that is often associated with dissolved marriages is financial problems. For the record, there hasn't been a single marriage in history that has ended because of finances. Surprised? Well, don't be.

The fact is, some marriages end because of *people's behavior* with money. It does not take a financial or relationship expert to figure out that individuals who engage in problematic financial behaviors are more likely to experience relationship difficulties.

So, where do you begin? You begin by taking a hard look at yourself. This means, evaluating your saving and spending habits, which is a reflection of your core values and general perception of life.

Here are several ways to simplify your financial life. First, have a plan. That is, live on a budget. Second, spend less than you earn. Third, save, save, save. Fourth, increase your income. Fifth, systematically pay off all debt and avoid new debt. Next, invest in good growth stock mutual funds. Finally, enjoy the fruits of your labor and wise investments.

I realize some of you aren't convinced winning at finances is this simple. Perhaps, you're right. But until you try this system, you really wouldn't know if it will or will not work. The fact is, this plan has worked for countless families across the globe.

Do yourself a favor; invest in your future and change your family tree by making wise financial decisions.

–The End –

Okay, to be honest, when I thought about writing this chapter on finances, I had ideas of getting really dramatic, and sharing real life horror stories of relationships that have gone down the dumps because neither partners were willing to act like grown ups and take responsibility for their financial indiscretions.

I would simply add that while you're dating,

if you realize that you and your partner have vastly different attitudes toward money, then it might be best to break off the relationship immediately, as it is likely to end in disaster.

Call the Cops

Ladies, please, please, please, I implore you to take the following seriously, because your life, or the life of a friend or family member might depend on it. Let me begin by defining domestic violence. Domestic violence is any form of unwanted physical force such as pushing, pinning, grabbing, pulling, holding, restraining or hitting, which causes physical discomfort, pain, injury, suffering or bodily harm.

The very first time, *not the second or third time*, but the very first time your partner, whether your husband, fiancé, or live-in companion, places his hands on you, in an attempt to control your actions, do not hesitate to get the law involved. Call the cops right away!

If you feel like it might be unsafe to call the police while he is in the house, make up an excuse to leave the house. The first opportunity you get to leave your house, go immediately to a police station, and report the abuse.

Here comes the hardest part. Do not return to the house where the abuse has been taking place. I know your kids are still in the house. I realize that there are many good memories there, but *your* life is worth so much more than memories. If you want to give your children a chance at a promising future, do what is best for them and get help for yourself.

Besides calling the cops and reporting the abuse, get everyone involved. Tell your neighbors. Tell every church member. Tell your girlfriends. Save and post pictures, share the story of the abuse on Facebook and other social media, and spread the word about this criminal.

By starting a campaign to make people aware of the physical abuse and trauma you are experiencing, the easier it will be for you to get out of that relationship, and start on the journey of self-restoration.

Here's where this message gets a little sticky. To my religious women, some of you might be wondering if it is right to leave your *religious* man if he physically abuses you. Heaven's YES!

First, domestic violence and abuse are not

spiritual problems. Secondly, you can't pray away your man's criminal behavior. Thirdly, an honorable man will never attempt to coerce or control his lady by using shame, guilt, physical force, or any other form of intimidation.

The question is not about whether it is right or wrong to leave or forgive an abusive man. The question is what is in your best physical, emotional, and spiritual interest, and also that of your children and other family members.

I encourage forgiveness, because it is the right thing to do. However, you should not stay in any relationship where you live in constant fear of being physically violated. You ought to leave that relationship. Let's remove any nuances from the word *leave*. Leave means to permanently set something aside, to give something up–no turning back. "Hasta la vista baby."

If you're married, should you get a divorce? Well, that's entirely up to you. What I'm saying is, you should not, under any circumstance, remain in any relationship where domestic violence and abuse are present.

Someone might be wondering how does the aforementioned factor in a situation where there has been only one incidence of physical aggression and violence.

Ladies, there is no such thing as *one* threatening or violent act. Yes, you lived through the first, and might have forgiven and moved on, but don't forget, you still live with the perpetrator. Although he told you that he's a changed man, and he'll never hit you again, you should not believe that lie. He will hit you again. It's just a matter of *when*.

The fact is: he is not a changed man. A physically abusive man will always be an abusive man. Right now, I imagine that some men might be pissed off at what I just stated. Remember buddy, you're the one who raised your hand on your woman–remember that!

Ladies, what I am saying is that not only is a man who physically abuses a woman, a punk, sissy and a coward, but also a man with serious emotional and mental issues. Your fasting and praying will not change him. Don't bother calling the church elders; they can't do anything for him. In fact, some of them are his friends, and there might be one or two of them who are guilty of the same crime against their spouses or girlfriends.

Ladies, an abusive relationship cannot be managed. You cannot rehabilitate a man who has decided to stoop to the vilest and lowest behavior among intelligent life forms. A physically abusive man cannot be fixed. Albeit, he can undergo lifetime counseling and anger management to get the healing that's needed to live a *normal* life. Even so, you do not need to be around while this savage brute undergoes therapy that offers no guarantee of producing long-term positive results.

Let's recap. I really did not intend to write more than a page on this subject. However, the urgency of this matter compelled me to go the extra mile, and if going the extra mile saves one woman's life, then it was worth it. Here are some facts to consider:

- Every 9 seconds in the US a woman is assaulted or beaten.
- Everyday in the US, more than three women are murdered by their husbands or boyfriends.
- At least one in every three women has been beaten, coerced into sex or otherwise abused during her lifetime. Most often, the abuser is a member of her own family.
- Nearly 1 in 5 teenage girls who have been in a relationship, said a boyfriend threatened

violence or self-harm if presented with a breakup.

- Domestic violence is the leading cause of injury to women–more than car accidents, muggings, and rapes combined.

Ladies, you owe it to yourself to live a life defined by happiness and one that is injury-free.

Social Media and Relationships

Anyone who has ever been in a relationship knows there are ups and downs, the good days and not so good days, trials and temptations, disappointment and regret, forgiveness and healing, and promise and adventure.

If you are in a relationship, then why not highlight what's working in your relationship, and stop sharing your filthy laundry on social media sites. If your relationship is as bad as you tell us, then get the hell out of it.

But to continue to talk about how insignificant your spouse or partner is speaks volumes about your character. You chose that person, with all his/her flaws—remember? "Oh, s/he changed." It could be that s/he changed because of you.

Think about this. Let's say you conclude that your relationship is not worth salvaging, then how are you preparing to meet the right person when all you're exposing to the world is that you're bitter, angry, unrestrained, tactless and imprudent.

What person in his or her right mind would want to be with you? Yes you're unhappy, but damn—stop rehearsing your problems on a public forum. Find the happiness you deserve. You'll be better for it.

Relational Intimacy

What is relational intimacy, and how is it achieved? The highest level of relational intimacy is achieved when I move beyond my own concerns, needs, and desires, and willingly, selflessly and genuinely submit to fulfilling the needs of my spouse without expecting and/or asking anything in return.

Relational intimacy rests on two pillars. The first pillar is *giving generously*. This idea implies going above and beyond what is requested or expected. The spirit of generosity anticipates the needs of your mate. That is, giving generously does not wait to be called on; rather, giving generously steps in to fulfill a need without being compelled. The spirit of generosity means to invest in small acts of service that add value to the relationship.

The second pillar of relational intimacy is *receiving gratefully*. A person who is vested in a committed relationship will find him or herself the recipient of many tokens of appreciation and tangible expressions of happiness. When you are the recipient of a generous gift from your partner, show your appreciation for your partner by accepting the gift gracefully and simply saying *thank you* with a smile.

When relational mutuality is balanced, relational intimacy comes to life. When I am willing to put myself last and go without so that my spouse can be fulfilled, I am participating in relational intimacy. When I am willing to accept tokens of grace in a spirit of humility, I am living in relational intimacy.

Psychology Application

Leveraging the Science of Relationships		
Concept	**Basic Premise**	**References**
The Matching Hypothesis	The matching hypothesis predicts that individuals on the dating market will assess their own self-worth and select partners whose social desirability approximately equals their own.	Taylor, L. S., Fiore, A. T., Mendelsohn, G. A., & Cheshire, C. (2011). "Out of my league": A real-world test of the matching hypothesis. *Personality and Social Psychology Bulletin*, 37(7), 942-954.
The Law of Propinquity	The law of propinquity states that the greater the physical (or psychological) proximity between people, the greater the chance that they will form friendships or romantic relationships.	**Theorists:** Leon Festinger, Stanley Schachter, and Kurt Back

Partner Selection	Adults seeking long-term relationships identify responsive caregiving qualities, such as attentiveness, warmth, and sensitivity, as most "attractive" in potential dating partners.	Hazan, C., & Selcuk, E. (2015). Normative Processes in Romantic Attachment: Introduction and Overview. In *Bases of Adult Attachment* (pp. 3-8). Springer New York.

Relationships and the Brain		
Concept	**Basic Premise**	**References**
The brain in love	Brain scans of both long-term and recent couples showed activity in the ventral tegmental area (VTA), an area with high **dopamine** concentration, which is associated with reward and motivation.	Dr. Melanie Greenberg in the *Mindful Self-Express*
Sex and the brain	Compared to new partners, long-term partners showed activity in brain areas associated with attachment that demonstrated greater calmness and less tension. Long-term partners may become more securely attached and less likely to fear abandonment. Higher sexual frequency was associated with greater activity in the **posterior hippocampus** –an area associated with hunger, cravings, and obsession.	**Theorist:** Dr. Melanie Greenberg

Brain Systems for Love		
Concept	**Basic Premise**	**References**
I love you with all my ~~heart~~; oops, I meant brain!	Regions of the brain associated with love. **ventral tegmental area, hypothalamus, nucleus accumbens,**	Sukel, K. (2012). *This is Your Brain On Sex: The Science Behind the Search for Love*. New York, NY: Simon & Schuster.
Lust	Lust stems predominantly from the **hypothalamus**, a region of the brain that also controls such basic desires as hunger and thirst.	Fisher, H. E., Aron, A., Mashek, D., Li, H., & Brown, L. L. (2002). Defining the brain systems of lust, romantic attraction, and attachment. *Archives of sexual behavior*, *31*(5), 413-419.
Sex drive	The sex drive (the libido or lust) is characterized by a craving for sexual gratification and it is associated primarily with the **estrogens** and **androgens** (female and male hormones respectively).	Ibid.

Part V: Self-Empowerment

Success demands constant attention. Success will reward you to the degree that you make it the center of your attention and affection. If you don't pay attention to success, it will treat you like a jealous girlfriend.

Success can be exhausting. Success does not care that you only got two hours of sleep. Success is not concerned about your doctor's or dentist appointment, or an emergency board meeting, Success is a full-time commitment. You're either fully on board or you're not.

Success does not show favoritism. Every child wants be his/her parents' favorite child. Every student wants to be highly regarded by the instructor. But success operates on a different plane. Success is indifferent to what one feels. Success cares about one thing and that is: can you replicate it—consistently.

Success reveals your true self. Success is not interested in your well-laid out plans regarding what you hope to achieve or become. Success does not care that your relationship and finances aren't together. Success wants to know that you will take advantage of an opportunity in the lifetime of the opportunity.

The power of success is cumulative, which means success favors success. That is why winners win and losers lose.

You can find yourself spending all of your time, energy and effort thinking about success and pursuing success without actually achieving success. The key to success is not in the doing but in the being.

Before you move full steam toward taking on success as a full-time endeavor, you need to have realistic expectations as to what you would like your life to be as it relates to your dreams, objectives and ambitions.

Be sure to consider the opportunity cost involved and also the desirable and undesirable consequences. If you select Option A, then what reward/opportunity are you passing up by not choosing Option B?

Remember this one thing about success and about life. Whatever you pour into the universe will be poured back into you with exponential force and intensity of time!

You Are Phenomenal!

When you woke up this morning, how much thought did you put into how you would like to spend the rest of your life? And if you have been giving consideration to your future, then the next question you should ask yourself is: "Am I doing enough?"

If you find yourself not "doing enough," then it could be that you are still struggling with self-doubt. There are moments when you might find yourself spending long periods in a persistent state of procrastination, fear and self-doubt. And that is natural. However, there comes a time when you must pick yourself up from the ashes and activate and unleash your creative powers.

You have a responsibility to live a life of purpose. I know it is tempting to remain on the sidelines. Sometimes you prefer to stay out of the limelight and remain hidden in the shadows.

Working behind the scenes might have become your new comfort zone.

But wouldn't it be great if the world got to meet you—the real YOU—the phenomenal person you really are?

You know, when I study success stories, one of the takeaways that immediately jumps right out at me is not the person who accomplished the impossible. No, no. I think about the person who passed up the opportunity to launch that great idea, product or service.

Take Uber for example, which is worth an estimated >$60 billion. Travis Kalanick and Garrett Camp turned a simple ride-sharing idea into a multi-billion dollar empire. They accomplished this feat against many odds. Here's the interesting part of this story. If Kalanick and Camp did not pursue this idea, do you think this concept would have remained trapped in the black hole of procrastination, doubt and regret? No! Someone else would have eventually brought the idea to market.

The same is true about the gifts that reside in you. Your gifts are waiting to burst forth. But they will not wait forever. If you do not give life to your passion(s), then rest assured that someone else will.

Someone is going to launch that beauty product that looks just like the one you couldn't stop thinking about—the product you should have launched. People are going to flock to the premiere of the movie, which is based on the book you should have written. Someone is going to build that million-dollar brand that reminds you of the same idea you allowed to remain dormant.

If you have turned silence, inaction and apathy into a profession and a way of life, then it is not too late to wake up from your slumber.

You know there is greatness inside you. And you have felt this way for some time. Instead of surrendering to self-doubt and procrastination, why not give yourself space and permission to blossom into something truly amazing. You are worth it!

Do Not Follow Your Passion...Unless You're Really Good At It

A common theme and idea shared by motivational speakers and the self-help circle is to *follow your passion*. I imagine that this recommendation comes from a good place and with good intent. Even so, is this mantra the best advice? Probably not.

Why do I say this? Well, here is why. If following your passion is the one missing ingredient that is supposed to take a person from living an average life to a phenomenal life, then why are so many people stuck between mediocrity and unfulfillment? Before I answer that question, here's what *I* mean by "follow your passion." Follow your passion simply means going after the things that will bring a high level of fulfillment. Now, back to the question.

The reason why it is not enough to simply follow your passion is because you might find yourself doing something you love, but not necessarily good at, which will inevitably lead to frustration.

Let's take the show American Idol as an example. Right before the contestants sing in front of the judges, they'd be interviewed in the waiting area and would be asked to tell the television audience a little about themselves and how they got into singing and so forth. More often than not, almost every contestant would speak of his or her passion and the love for music and singing. A few minutes later, those same individuals would get on the stage—and noise that came out of their mouths sounded like the combination of a train coming to a screeching stop and a wounded animal—just horrendous.

Now, does this mean that a person should not follow his or her passion? Of course not. What I am saying is if you are following your passion but are getting nowhere, then something is wrong. Passion is a good starting point, but it is not enough. The key to living a fulfilled life is to find and employ the right combination of passion, skill, need and impact.

That is, there needs to be a balance between: (1) what you are passionate about; (2) what you are really skilled at doing; (3) what your skill can do for others—meaning, does your skill, gift or talent offer a unique solution to a real problem; (4) and the level and number of people you impact.

Look around you. Study the lives of those who are winning and you will notice a common theme. Winners are not only passionate about their craft, but they are also really really good at what they do. You'd also notice that winners have the right set of skills to address a specific opportunity in the market place.

So, perhaps it is time for you to move on and try something else. But, how do you find your passion? My philosophy is that the best way to find your passion is to try different and new things until you get there.

To recap, I am all in for passion. But if your passion only benefits you, then you might want to recalibrate your moral compass. Your passion should be so irresistible, so dynamic and so compelling that all it does is add value to people's lives on a wide scale—continually.

Execution Is Worshiped!

Everybody wants to win. Everyone wants a piece of the pie. Everybody wants to make it big. Everyone wants to enjoy unparalleled success. People yearn to live a life that bears some semblance of accomplishment. Every person has a mental picture of his or her successful self. BUT very few people *execute* in order to win!

Why is this? How is it that a person can be consciously aware that by implementing a series of actions, success is inevitable, yet does not take any steps to make the image of the *successful self* a reality? Is the *fear of failure* a limiting factor? Could it be that people wait for *concrete evidence* that their plans will succeed rather than working to ensure their plans succeed?

Let's briefly examine these two factors: *fear of failure* and *concrete evidence*. Regarding the fear of failure, I get it. No one wants his or her life to be viewed as a grand joke. No one wants to be an epic failure. No one wants to be a bust, especially in a culture that lauds success as a most important human value.

The reality is, failure is a part of life. And the sooner you accept that, the better able and prepared you'll be to execute smart actionable strategies that will serve your long-term interests. Another great thing about failure is that failure allows success to reveal itself.

Regarding the *concrete evidence* factor, success should not be pursued based on tangible proof that an idea will work out. Sometimes, the plans we're most confident will work, flops. And other times we're surprised by the forward momentum produced by other less-considered ideas. The point is, winning should be as fun as it is unpredictable, and you should be flexible and adaptable—and enjoy the process.

The most important aspect as it relates to executing your goals is to execute your goals. Your focus should be on execution because execution can lead to extraordinary results. Don't believe me? Well, just ask Bevel's Tristan Walker, Twitter's Evan Williams and Jack Dorsey, Netflix's Reed Hastings, Amazon's Jeff Bezos, TaskRabbit's Leah Busque, Virgin's Sir Richard Branson, Travis

Kalanick and Garrett Camp of Uber, Brian Chesky, Joe Gebbia and Nathan Blecharczyk of Airbnb, Facebook's Mark Zukerberg, and Scholly's Christopher Gray.

Here's the final facet of *execution* that I'd like you to consider. When executing, you want to be sure that you are aiming at a specific and carefully selected target. Too broad of an execution strategy could result in missing every target. So, choose that plan, product or service that has the greatest potential to disrupt and revolutionize an industry and drive sustainable financial impact.

In essence, your execution has to be consistent with your vision and commitment to winning. Winning individuals and winning brands execute, and do so consistently and in manner that gives them a competitive advantage. Remember there is no winning unless there is first execution.

You Owe It To Yourself To...

Most people will only experience marginal success in life because the behavior or action that is most likely to produce the outcome (success) they desire is not positively reinforced frequently and consistently.

For example, the less wins a person experiences, the less motivated that person becomes as it relates to engaging in life-changing opportunities. But the more wins you accumulate, the more likely you will engage in the activities that produce the wins. Hence the saying: ***Winners win and losers lose.***

In essence, we become what we listen to on a regular basis. We become what we read on a regular basis. We become what we watch on a regular basis. But most importantly, we become what we do!

So, what are you listening to? What are you watching? What are you reading? In what ways are those activities adding value to your life? Or, is what you're doing distracting you and keeping you in a perpetual state of mediocrity? What are you doing that will elevate you to unparalleled success?

You owe it to yourself to be happier than you've ever being. You owe it to yourself to have more money than you have ever had. You owe it to yourself to achieve more than you've ever achieved. You owe it to yourself to go where you've never been before. You owe it to yourself to love and be loved like you've never experienced. You owe it to yourself to serve like you've never served.

Pause, stop and self-assess. Take time to live like no one else today so that you can live like no one else in the future. You owe it to yourself to live a phenomenal life!

Don't Forget To Do These Things Before Going To Bed

Do you know what successful people do right before they go to bed? They read, write, and reflect. That is, they absorb inspiration relating to their craft, which is their way of picturing or capturing tomorrow's success.

By engaging in those three activities, successful people are better able to identify: how much progress they are making as it relates to their goals; what direction they want to pursue; and what they need to do to accomplish their goals.

So many, too many people go through life thinking, hoping and praying that success opportunities will yield to them based on good intentions. I imagine that broke people have good intentions, but they're still broke. Having good intentions regarding success is meaningless unless action accompanies those intentions. Successful people are always several steps ahead of the game and they never allow tomorrow to catch them unprepared. This mindset, this lifestyle is one of the determining factors that separate successful people from everyone else.

The reality is, no one stumbles into success. Success has to be studied carefully and thoroughly before it can be mastered and earned. So, do yourself a favor and take a few minutes before bed each night to envision how you would like to spend the rest of your life.

I'll Just Watch You Drown

Allow me to jump right in. Do you know why most people will never become successful?

No, it's not because they do not have a goal, vision or plan. It's not that they fear success or lack motivation, discipline or knowledge. It's not even because they're lazy, entitled, negative, make excuses, waste time, think too small, do not believe, spend too much time on social media, listen to the wrong information, hang around losers, distracted, or don't execute.

I was sixteen years old—having fun at the beach with a bunch of friends from church, in the Virgin Islands where I was born and raised. I will never forget that fateful Sunday. Like most enterprising and adventurous teenagers, we all thought we were invincible. So, it happened that while we (the boys) were standing on the shore talking about which of the many pretty girls we liked and would love to go out with, we came up with a plan that we thought would impress the girls.

Our grand and audacious idea was to throw a floating object as far as we could into the water, and the guy who swam to the object and brought it back first would get to go on a date with one of those charming princesses. The girls went along with our plan and promised that the guy who successfully accomplished the task would be the happiest teenager in history (wink, wink). Okay, it's not what you're thinking. These girls were level-headed and were not easily enticed or ensnared.

Anyway, although I was an average swimmer at best, I decided to participate in the contest because my eyes were set on the most beautiful girl on the beach that day. Her name was Stephanie. I had to win—I needed Stephanie to see how dauntless and valorous I was.

"On your mark, get set, go!" someone shouted. We dove into the water and swam like mad men over and through the waves toward the floating object. All I could think about as I swam to the illusive object was Stephanie. Although most of the guys who competed were incredible swimmers—no one was going to beat me that day. I was determined to win, and I did. I didn't reach the object first; however, the few guys who got to the object before I did were busy jostling for position, and while they were busy fending off each other, I dove underneath them and surfaced with object in my hand. The girls on the beach screamed in excitement—cheering on the victor, yours truly.

Some of the losers swam to an island of rocks about one hundred yards away while the other dispirited guys swam back to shore. I had accomplished half of the challenge. And the next half was to bring the prize to the ladies. With the object in my hand, I started swimming to shore. Then I realized something. The shore was really, really far away—and the people looked really tiny. During my mad dash, I didn't realized how far out I had swam. Remember, I was an average swimmer.

Well, I started swimming back to shore, and for some reason the shore was not getting any closer. So, I took it up a notch and kicked harder and gave it everything I had. But in doing so, I ran out of energy halfway to the shore. I felt myself starting to panic, but I did some positive self-talk, which bought me a half-a-minute of energy. But those seconds passed by quickly and my arms started to feel like stones and my legs stopped kicking altogether. I was about to drown right in front of all of my new female fans—but my fans were no longer paying attention to me. They'd quickly forgotten about me and were eating, listening to music, and having fun.

When you're staring death in the face, you can do two things. You can accept the inevitability of it, or you can choose to fight. I chose the latter. I told myself that I wanted to live, more than I wanted to die. In those seconds, which seemed like an eternity, I felt as if I were having a conversation with the Grim Reaper himself. And I told him "Not today, buddy. First, I am not drowning in front of my friends and fans. And secondly, I am determined to go on a date with Stephanie. So keep moving."

Wouldn't you know it—I found new life and energy. And I darted toward the shore, which was still quite a distance away. But the trouble wasn't over yet. Once again, I flamed out. However, I flamed out right next to a friend of mine who saw that I was in trouble and was watching me the entire time.

She swam to me and jokingly said, "Joe, you don't seem to be doing okay."

To which I responded, "I don't think I'll make it to the shore, can you help me?"

"Let me think about it," she said.

"Please," I begged.

Her face lit up like the sun that was bearing down on us. "You gotta go on a date with me," she replied. "And you can't go out with Stephanie."

She knew I liked Stephanie.

"Not happening," I rebutted.

"Fine, then I guess I'll just watch you drown."

I felt the blood drain from my face. "Okay, okay, I'll do anything."

She smirked. "Define *anything*."

"I'll go on a date with you," I hollered, with what I thought would be my last breath.

This guardian angel kept her word and allowed me to rest my hand on her shoulder as she towed me in to shore, where I collapsed from sheer exhaustion. After regaining my energy and bearings, I sought out my new angel and told her that I planned on keeping my word. She told me that she was kidding, and encouraged me to go out with Stephanie. She even gave me a few pointers.

Here's the heart of the matter. Most people will never become successful because of one simple reason—they don't want success badly enough! Unless you want success as badly as you want to breathe, then you'll never be successful. On that day when I was faced with the odds of choosing between life or drowning—I chose Stephanie!

You, my friend, are endowed with everything you need to succeed at the highest levels! So, why not take a chance on success and see what your life could be.

A Fate Worse Than Death

Can you think of anything worse than death?

There might be some of you who can create an exhaustive list right off the cuff while others might need a bit more time to come up with a list. Well, I did a Google search of the phrase "what's worse than death" and here's what I found. Some of the examples included: chronic illness, quadriplegia, torture, taxes, poverty, loving the wrong person, divorce, life, and immortality.

Taxes? Really? I can't imagine how taxes are worse than death. And immortality? This one puzzled me. How can anyone view immortality as being worse than death? Yes, I get the loneliness, watching loved-ones die, monotony, etc. Even so, I'd accept the gift of immortality any day of the week. But, I guess to each his or her own, right?

Anyway, here's what I had in mind regarding the topic. When I think of a fate worse than death, the first thought that comes to mind is *living a wasted life*. Why would *living a wasted life* be a fate worse than death? Here's my two-word answer: *human potential*. Yes, "human potential"—meaning, the plow, the ship, the wheel, the compass, the printing press, the steam engine, the automobile, the internal combustion engine, the telephone, the light bulb, refrigeration, penicillin, the airplane & helicopter, contraceptives, the computer, the Internet, the smart phone, the Ultimate Expression.

What if there were ten, just ten additional inventors throughout history—ten people who would have dug deeper, trusted their gut instincts, ignored the noise, e.g., skeptics/haters/dream-killers, and followed their hearts as it relates to that invention that never saw the light of day? Perhaps we would have already solved poverty and world hunger and climate change. It could be that we would have already colonized distant planets. Conceivably, cancer, heart disease and diabetes would have been things of the past. Just, what if?

Why have life if you're not going to *live*? Why make the conscious decision to descend into nothingness—to live a life absent of purpose?

The truth is, in life, you never really know if the path that you're on will lead to success. But *not knowing* should never be an excuse for inaction. Too many people have made sacrifices for you to be where you're at right now. It might have been your mom and dad, or a mentor or friend who made it possible for you to have a shot at a better life. Don't those people deserve a better return on their investment than the effort you're currently putting forth? For those of us living in the United States of America—I mean, what greater place to pursue our dreams.

So, yes, there is a fate worse than death, and that's living a wasted life. But you and I do not have to accept or participate in that existence. We can decide to sacrifice temporary pleasures, instant gratification, even our time, sleep, stability and health in order to win—in order to change our family tree and leave a lasting legacy.

Motivated To Do Something You Love

What is the last thing you think about before going to bed? And what is the first thing you think about when you wake up?

Are the two thoughts related? How do those thoughts fit into your daily schedule? Are they related to your job or career? If those thoughts/activities are not linked to your livelihood, then perhaps you need to pause and ask yourself, "why?"

What if the goal, dream, or passion you go to bed thinking about is the path or goal you should be pursuing on a full-time basis? Why else would you be thinking about mathematical modeling right before you go to bed and as soon as wake up? Could it be that you belong in a STEM field? Possibly.

If the thought that is consuming your mind late at nights and early mornings is that important to you, then why not pursue it? Why can't your job/career and dreams co-exist? Better yet, why can't they be one and the same.

Think about the following for a moment. Are you motivated by your job/career? Do you brag about how great your company is and what a wonderful life your job allows you to have? —You know, the great salary, the stock options, the paid four-week vacation, the awesome health benefits, the quarterly bonuses, free membership to the company's clubhouse. Or does the thought of your job turn into a negative feeling?

Why spend the few years that you have been given engaging in activities that do not bring you happiness and complete satisfaction? Why live the rest of your life bending to the will of an employer—building their brand and growing their financial portfolio?

But does this mean abandoning your present realities of providing for your family and saving for your retirement to pursue an enchanted path of bliss? Absolutely not. What I'm saying is, why not build a career doing something you love. You're already thinking about *it*. And you're motivated by *it* because the universe chose you to live and experience *it* —whatever *it* is.

Nobody Cares About Your Story Until You Win

In one of his motivational videos, motivational guru and sensation, Dr. Eric Thomas made a statement that gave me pause. He said: "Nobody cares about your story until you win." I thought, "Hmmm, is that really true?" I have since had some time to ponder on that statement and here are my thoughts. First, I'm not sure if I would go as far as saying that "nobody cares." I prefer to believe that some people do care, but most people simply aren't interested in your story. And there's a legitimate reason as to why they are not interested.

The context of Eric's assertion is that it is not until you take your own life seriously that others will take you seriously. Think about the family member or friend who has been telling you for the last few months or years how s/he is about to blow up—how s/he is going to make it onto the big stage. You want to be positive, but deep down you know that person is full of hot air and what you're hearing is mostly fluff.

Here's the connection. If you want the world to pay attention to what you are doing, then you need to do something truly significant—something spectacular! Regardless of the form of delivery—whether it is a product or service, you must be able to capture people's heart and imagination. Your product/service must tell a story and solve an unsolvable problem. "An unsolvable problem," you ask? "There is no such thing," you say. Well, there is. And those people who have found a way to offer temporary solutions to unsolvable problems are the headliners—they make the front-page news—they're what's trending.

So, what's an unsolvable problem? Hunger and thirst and two examples of an unsolvable problem. Think about it. When you are hungry, you get something to eat. And when you are thirsty, you find something to drink. But do the food and drink "solve" hunger and/or thirst? No, the food and beverage only provide a temporary solution. Here's the clincher. The people or brands that tell a compelling story and offer a unique "solution" to our presenting "unsolvable" problems are the brands we patronize—e.g., Starbucks, Coke, Pepsi, Subway, McDonald's, Pizza Hut, Papa Johns, Popeyes, KFC, Outback Steakhouse, Olive Garden, Applebees, The Cheesecake Factory.

Those companies understand that they cannot solve the hunger and thirst problem; however, they know that if they offer a unique product/service that could capture your imagination, you are likelier than not to participate in their story by opening your purses and wallets.

So, if you want to experience unparalleled success—if you want the world to pay attention to what you're doing—if you want to be a headliner-the main act on the grand stage, then you need to do something truly special. Your company—YOU must create a one-of-a-kind experience and solution to an *unsolvable* problem.

Go Fund Me_The New Hustle

There is hardly a week that goes by on social media without seeing a new crowd funding campaign. The rise of this new form of panhandling is probably the result of one of two things—either the universe has increased our share of personal problems, struggles and difficulties at a dramatically alarming rate and exponential level OR technology has simply made it easier for some people to approach complete strangers and beg rather than work out their self-inflicted financial woes.

Of course, there are legitimate and unexpected problems that can blindside the most prepared, such as illness, accident, or death. But most of these campaigns are not seeking money for the aforementioned examples or to launch a business. Conversely, these campaigns have become nothing more than self-serving *take care of my entitled lazy ass* hustles.

People are literally asking others to sponsor, fund and pay for their weddings, their vacations, their college/university tuition, rent, vehicle payment, lifestyle, hobbies and dreams.

Go Fund Me (not the company but crowd funding) has become the new hustle!

So, let's get this straight. You made the choice to spend like Members of Congress and live above your means, and now you are asking me to foot the bill—the bills YOU created due to years of fiscal irresponsibility? I am supposed to use my hard-earned money to sponsor your habits—the habits of an adult-child? Are you freaking kidding me?

You know, **there was a time when it was okay to struggle**. There was a time when struggling to make ends meet was not a bad thing—of course, I am referring to those whose struggles were real— those folks working several jobs, and living on a budget just to get by—that type of struggle. There was a time when it was okay not to have every desired amenity and luxury. There was a time when it was okay to live in a tiny one-bedroom apartment, and move up in house size as the family (and earnings) grew.

There was a time when it was okay not to be driving the latest model vehicle. There was a time when it was perfectly fine to work at a minimum wage job then climb your way up the earnings ladder. There was a time when it was okay to work and go to school at the same time. There was a time when it was okay not to be cool.

There was a time when people's first thought when facing a difficult situation was not to beg or ask for a handout; rather, people's first impulse when facing a difficulty was to GRIND their way out of the said difficulty. There was a time when people took pride in funding their own dreams through the 'painstaking' process of planning, preparation and smart and hard work.

Studies show that domesticating wild animals can harm their survival instinct—leading to ecological imbalance. The same is true for human beings. When you take the struggle out of life, it demoralizes the will and weakens the person.

So, please do all of us a favor and stop begging! Get a job or two. Better yet, get a life. If I have to work to get mine, so should you. Remember, anything worth having is worth pursuing—through grit, determination and effort, and most importantly—through hard work!

You Do Deserve Life's Best

In order to experience the life you deserve, you MUST free your mind from the idea that you are not worthy or less deserving than anyone else.

Each time you tell yourself that you are not worthy, you are accepting defeat. Every time you feel that you are less deserving than anyone else, you are giving others permission to dictate the outcomes of your life. There will always be someone who is more educated than you – someone with more money, nicer things, bigger house, fancier car, better looking partner/spouse, or more social capital (clout).

So what? It is not the accumulation of stuff that makes a person important, special or successful. Your success and happiness have everything to do with the way you perceive yourself. The way you perceive yourself is the way others see and treat you. If you perceive and treat yourself as the queen or king you are, then people will treat you as royalty.

Many people say that the most important aspect of the human existence is the ability to live. Life is indeed a gift. Even so, I maintain that the most important currency of the human experience is the ability to love – self-love. It is out of the love for self that other forms and acts of love become possible.

So, pay no attention to the naysayers. In fact, tell them "go to hell." Concentrate on your strengths rather than your limitations. Focus on your powers instead of your problems. Let the life you want become the reality you live.

About the Author

JOSIAH SAMUEL HARRY currently serves as a university lecturer, educational consultant, and success coach/mentor. Josiah's research interests are in humanistic philosophy, social change and counterculture. Josiah was born and raised in St. Croix, U.S. Virgin Islands. He holds earned degrees in sociology, religion, psychology and business.

"Aha" Moments

Day 1:

_____
_____
_____
_____
_____
_____
_____

Day 2:

_____
_____
_____
_____
_____
_____
_____

Day 3:

_____

_____

_____

_____

_____

_____

_____

Day 4:

_____

_____

_____

_____

_____

_____

_____

Day 5:

_____

_____

_____

_____

_____

_____

_____

Day 6:

_____

_____

_____

_____

_____

_____

_____

Day 7:

_____
_____
_____
_____
_____
_____
_____
_____

Day 8:

_____
_____
_____
_____
_____
_____
_____
_____

Day 9:

_____

_____

_____

_____

_____

_____

_____

Day 10:

_____

_____

_____

_____

_____

_____

_____

Day 11:

_____
_____
_____
_____
_____
_____
_____
_____

Day 12:

_____
_____
_____
_____
_____
_____
_____
_____

Day 13:

_____

_____

_____

_____

_____

_____

_____

Day 14:

_____

_____

_____

_____

_____

_____

_____

Day 15:

_____

_____

_____

_____

_____

_____

_____

Day 16:

_____

_____

_____

_____

_____

_____

_____

Day 17:

_____

_____

_____

_____

_____

_____

_____

_____

Day 18:

_____

_____

_____

_____

_____

_____

_____

_____

Day 19:

_____

_____

_____

_____

_____

_____

_____

_____

Day 20:

_____

_____

_____

_____

_____

_____

_____

Day 21:

_____

_____

_____

_____

_____

_____

_____

You Got Next!

_____

_____

_____

_____

_____

_____

_____

Budget Worksheet

CATEGORY	MONTHLY BUDGET AMOUNT	MONTHLY ACTUAL AMOUNT	DIFFERENCE
INCOME:			
Wages and Bonuses			
Interest Income			
Investment Income			
Miscellaneous Income			
Income Subtotal			
INCOME TAXES WITHHELD:			
Federal Income Tax			
State and Local Income Tax			
Social Security/Medicare Tax			
Income Taxes Subtotal			
Spendable Income			
EXPENSES:			
HOME:			
Mortgage or Rent			
Homeowners/Renters Insurance			
Property Taxes			

Home Repairs/Maintenance/HOA Dues			
Home Improvements			
Household Products			

CATEGORY	MONTHLY BUDGET AMOUNT	MONTHLY ACTUAL AMOUNT	DIFFERENCE
UTILITIES:			
Electricity			
Water and Sewer			
Natural Gas or Oil			
Telephone (Land Line, Cell)			
Internet			
FOOD:			
Groceries			
Eating Out, Lunches, Snacks			
FAMILY OBLIGATIONS:			
Day Care, Babysitting			
Child Support			
Alimony			
HEALTH AND MEDICAL:			
Insurance - medical, dental, vision			
Unreimbursed Medical Expenses, Copays			
Fitness (Yoga, Massage, Gym)			
TRANSPORTATION:			
Car Payments			
Gasoline/Oil			
Auto Repairs/Maintenance/ Fees			
Auto Insurance			

Other Transportation (tolls, bus, subway, taxis)			

CATEGORY	MONTHLY BUDGET AMOUNT	MONTHLY ACTUAL AMOUNT	DIFFERENCE
DEBT PAYMENTS:			
Credit Cards			
Student Loans			
Other Loans			
ENTERTAINM ENT/RECREAT ION:			
Cable TV/Videos/Movi es			
Computer Expense			
Hobbies			
Subscriptions and Dues			
Vacations			
PETS:			
Food			
Grooming, Boarding, Vet			
CLOTHING:			
INVESTMENTS AND SAVINGS:			
401(K) or IRA			
Stocks/Bonds/Mu tual Funds			
College Fund			
Savings			
Emergency Fund			
MISCELLANE OUS:			
Gifts/Donations			
Grooming (Hair, Make-up, Other)			
Total Investments and Expenses			

Surplus or Shortage (Spendable income minus total expenses and investments)			

For expenses incurred more or less often than monthly, convert the payment to a monthly amount when calculating the monthly budget. For instance, convert auto expense that's billed every six months to a monthly amount by dividing the six-month premium by six. This money should be kept separate from your other money so it's available when the bill becomes due.[8]

---

[8] http://financialplan.about.com/cs/budgeting/l/blbudget.htm